Mastering The Faster Web with PHP, MySQL, and JavaScript

Develop state-of-the-art web applications using the latest web technologies

Andrew Caya

BIRMINGHAM - MUMBAI

Mastering The Faster Web with PHP, MySQL, and JavaScript

Commissioning Editor: Amarabha Banerjee
Acquisition Editor: Shweta Pant
Content Development Editor: Mohammed Yusuf Imaratwale
Technical Editor: Akhil Nair
Copy Editor: Safis Editing
Project Coordinator: Hardik Bhinde
Proofreader: Safis Editing
Indexer: Pratik Shirodkar
Graphics: Jason Monteiro
Production Coordinator: Aparna Bhagat

First published: June 2018

Production reference: 1060618

Published by Packt Publishing Ltd.
Livery Place
35 Livery Street
Birmingham
B3 2PB, UK.

ISBN 978-1-78839-221-1

www.packtpub.com

I dedicate this book to the One who has made everything new by His sacrifice and has given me everything that I have in my life.

To my wife, Mylène, and my son, Jean-Thomas, whom I love very much, for their relentless support and understanding.

To my extended family, Andrée-Anne, Geneviève, Marie-Rose and Augustin, for their trust and confidence in me.

To my mother, Lise, and my father, Carroll, may he rest in peace, for everything that they have taught and given me over the years.

To all my friends, particularly Martin, Élise, Rose-Anne, and Martin, for their patience and collaboration.

To my computer science instructors, Richard Truchon, Jean-Marie Veilleux, Daryl Wood, and Jakub Zalas, who have made me the computer programmer that I am today, with a very special mention to Doug Bierer, whose good mentoring and true friendship changed my professional life forever.

`mapt.io`

Mapt is an online digital library that gives you full access to over 5,000 books and videos, as well as industry leading tools to help you plan your personal development and advance your career. For more information, please visit our website.

Why subscribe?

- Spend less time learning and more time coding with practical eBooks and Videos from over 4,000 industry professionals

- Improve your learning with Skill Plans built especially for you

- Get a free eBook or video every month

- Mapt is fully searchable

- Copy and paste, print, and bookmark content

PacktPub.com

Did you know that Packt offers eBook versions of every book published, with PDF and ePub files available? You can upgrade to the eBook version at `www.PacktPub.com` and as a print book customer, you are entitled to a discount on the eBook copy. Get in touch with us at `service@packtpub.com` for more details.

At `www.PacktPub.com`, you can also read a collection of free technical articles, sign up for a range of free newsletters, and receive exclusive discounts and offers on Packt books and eBooks.

Foreword

At first glance, my initial instinct was to wonder, "why am I reading yet another book on web development?" After all, I've been in the business for so long that I've learned to say, when asked how many years of experience, over 30. What more is there to learn, right? Wrong! First of all, I'm sure deep down in your gut you'll agree that no matter how long you've been in the business, there is always something new to be learned. This is where our friend Andrew Caya comes in.

Andrew is and has been my best student. He's the only one to have attended all the courses I teach for Zend, and also to have purchased all the books and videos I've done for O'Reilly and Packt. Okay, Okay, I can almost hear you muttering to yourself that maybe the guy's crazy, has no control over his spending habits. Well not to worry: his wife has things firmly under control, and his credit cards are currently under house arrest.

So ... What about Andrew? Aside from the fact that he not only has a deep understanding of new and existing technologies, he's thorough and tries things out, which is a refreshing departure from many authors who "talk the talk," but do not "walk the walk."

What deeply impressed me about this book, however, and made me realize that it contains essential information for any web developer, no matter how experienced, is how Andrew has taken a deep dive not only into new technologies, but very cleverly brought to light aspects of the existing technologies as well. After reading just the first few chapters, I learned things about PHP and benchmarking that I did not realize existed, even having used such tools since their inception. Another example is found in his last chapter, *Beyond Performance*. Here, Andrew offers masterful insights such as pointing out that the traditional way of viewing performance itself might be an issue, which then leads into a discussion of UI design and user perception.

In this book, Andrew presents the concepts clearly and concisely. He also shows you how to install, configure, and then put to use the various tools and techniques which, combined, will result in better web performance, that is, the Faster Web. There are plenty of screenshots where the various controls, settings, and expected outcomes are meticulously highlighted. I won't bore you with the extensive list of technologies, tools, and techniques Andrew covers, but let me tell you that there's some really exciting stuff here that will ultimately put you in charge of your website and its development.

Be honest with yourself: do you experience a pang of dread whenever the phone rings, hoping against hope that it's not another customer complaint? Do you find yourself running ragged chasing down bugs? Are you really looking forward to spending yet another weekend at the office eating cold pizza? Andrew's book will turn your life around and "put you back in the driver's seat," as the saying goes. If you apply the concepts and use the tools he describes, you might even start enjoying your job and be able to use all the unused paid leave you've accumulated. Treat yourself to this book and enjoy your day in the sun!

Doug Bierer

unlikelysource.com

P.S. If you're like me and like to poke fun at the hard-core "Test Driven Development" nerds, have a look at Andrew's chapter entitled Javascript and "Danger-Driven Development".

Contributors

About the author

Andrew Caya started programming computers in GW-BASIC and QBASIC in the early 90s. Before becoming a PHP developer almost 10 years ago, he did some software development in C, C++, and Perl. He is now a Zend Certified PHP Engineer and a Zend Certified Architect. He is also the creator of *Linux for PHP*, the lead developer of a popular Joomla extension and a contributor to many open source projects.

He is currently CEO, CTO and Founder of *Foreach Code Factory*, an instructor at *Concordia University*, an author and a technical reviewer for *Packt Publishing*, and a loving husband and father.

I wish to thank Packt Publishing for offering me this great opportunity, the entire editorial team and the technical reviewers for their valued help on this project, Doug Bierer for his kind support throughout the project, Cal Evans and Nomad PHP for their professional training, and my family and friends for their ever-renewed enthusiasm.

About the reviewers

Federico Kereki is a Uruguayan Systems Engineer, with a Masters Degree in Education, and over 30 years' experience as a consultant, developer, professor, and writer.

He is a Subject Matter Expert at Globant, and he has taught at *Universidad de la República*, *Universidad ORT*, and *Universidad de la Empresa*.

He has written several articles for magazines and web sites, a pair of booklets on computer security, and two books: *Essential GWT* and *Mastering JavaScript Functional Programming*. He's currently writing a new book on JavaScript development for Packt Publishing.

Jakub Zalas is an independent software consultant, architect and trainer, who helps teams to deliver software that survives change. Being focused on quality, Jakub promotes agile development practices, like test driven development. In his spare time, he speaks at conferences and contributes to open source.

Packt is searching for authors like you

If you're interested in becoming an author for Packt, please visit `authors.packtpub.com` and apply today. We have worked with thousands of developers and tech professionals, just like you, to help them share their insight with the global tech community. You can make a general application, apply for a specific hot topic that we are recruiting an author for, or submit your own idea.

Table of Contents

Preface

The Faster Web can be defined as a series of qualities to be developed in all spheres of web technology in order to speed up any transaction between a client and a server. It also includes the principles behind UI design that can influence a user's perception of speed. Thus, understanding the Faster Web involves understanding the notions of performance, efficiency and perceived performance, and discovering most of the new underlying web technologies that make up what the internet has become today.

Who this book is for

Any web developer, system administrator or web enthusiast who wishes to understand the Faster Web better. Basic knowledge of *Docker* container technology is a plus.

What this book covers

Chapter 1, *Faster Web – Getting Started*, defines what is the Faster Web by trying to better understand the formal aspects of it and sets out to understand how to measure performance and determine if a website or Web application is part of the Faster Web or not.

Chapter 2, *Continuous Profiling and Monitoring*, aims to help the reader learn how to install and configure profiling and monitoring tools that will help them easily optimize PHP code in a continuous integration (CI) and a **continuous deployment** (**CD**) environment.

Chapter 3, *Harnessing the Power of PHP 7 Data Structures and Functions*, gets the reader to learn how to harness PHP 7's performance boosts through most of its key optimizations. It also helps them explore how better understanding data structures and data types, and using simplified functions can help a PHP application's global performance along its critical execution path. In addition, it covers how it is best to avoid using inefficient structures, like most dynamic ones, in our PHP code, and how some functional techniques can be of immediate help when optimizing PHP code.

Chapter 4, *Envisioning the Future with Asynchronous PHP*, outlines how to cope with input and output (I/O) poor latency by learning about generators and asynchronous non-blocking code, multithreading with the *POSIX Threads* (`pthreads`) library and multitasking with the `ReactPHP` library.

Chapter 5, *Measuring and Optimizing Database Performance,* shows how to measure database performance, ranging from simple measurement techniques to advanced benchmarking tools.

Chapter 6, *Querying Efficiently a Modern SQL Database,* explains how to use Modern SQL techniques in order to optimize complex SQL queries.

Chapter 7, *JavaScript and Danger-Driven Development,* covers a few of JavaScript's best and worst parts, especially those that pertain to code efficiency and overall performance, and how a developer should always write safe, reliable and highly efficient JavaScript code, mostly by avoiding "danger-driven development".

Chapter 8, *Functional JavaScript,* features how JavaScript is becoming more and more a functional language and how this programming paradigm will be a vector for performance in the near future by taking a quick look at upcoming language features that will help improve performance of JavaScript applications.

Chapter 9, *Boosting a Web Server's Performance,* looks at what the HTTP/2 protocol is all about and how the SPDY project made it possible, how PHP-FPM and OPcache can help you boost the performance of your PHP scripts, how to use ESI technology by setting up a Varnish Cache server, how to use client-side caching and how other Faster Web tools can help you boost a web server's overall performance.

Chapter 10, *Going Beyond Performance,* shows how, when everything seems to have been fully optimized, we can still go beyond performance by better understanding the principles behind UI design when it comes to the perception of performance.

To get the most out of this book

In order to run the source code included in this book, we recommend that you start by installing Docker on your computer (https://docs.docker.com/engine/installation/). *Docker* is a software container platform that allows you to easily connect to your computer's devices in an isolated and sophisticated chroot-like environment. Unlike virtual machines, containers do not come bundled with full operating systems, but only come with the required binaries in order to run some software. You can install *Docker* on Windows, Mac, or Linux. It should be noted, however, that some features, such as full-featured networking, are still not available when running *Docker* on macOS (https://docs.docker.com/docker-for-mac/networking/#known-limitations-use-cases-and-workarounds).

The main *Docker* image that we will be using throughout this book is *Linux for PHP* 8.1 (`https://linuxforphp.net/`) with a non thread-safe version of PHP 7.1.16 and *MariaDB* (*MySQL*) 10.2.8 (asclinux/linuxforphp-8.1:7.1.16-nts). To start the main container, enter the following command:

```
# docker run --rm -it \
> -v ${PWD}/:/srv/fasterweb \
> -p 8181:80 \
> asclinux/linuxforphp-8.1:7.1.16-nts \
> /bin/bash
```

If you prefer using multithreading technologies while optimizing your code, you can do so by running a thread-safe version of *Linux for PHP* (asclinux/linuxforphp-8.1:7.0.29-zts).

Moreover, you should `docker commit` any changes you make to the container and create new images of your container that you can `docker run` at a later time. If you are not familiar with the Docker command line and its `run` command, find the documentation at `https://docs.docker.com/engine/reference/run/`.

Finally, the three following commands must be run inside the Linux for PHP container whenever you start an original Linux for PHP image and wish to start working with most of the code examples contained in this book:

```
# /etc/init.d/mysql start
# /etc/init.d/php-fpm start
# /etc/init.d/httpd start
```

Download the example code files

You can download the example code files for this book from your account at `www.packtpub.com`. If you purchased this book elsewhere, you can visit `www.packtpub.com/support` and register to have the files emailed directly to you.

You can download the code files by following these steps:

1. Log in or register at `www.packtpub.com`
2. Select the **SUPPORT** tab
3. Click on **Code Downloads & Errata**
4. Enter the name of the book in the **Search** box and follow the onscreen instructions

Once the file is downloaded, please make sure that you unzip or extract the folder using the latest version of:

- WinRAR/7-Zip for Windows
- Zipeg/iZip/UnRarX for Mac
- 7-Zip/PeaZip for Linux

The code bundle for the book is also hosted on GitHub at `https://github.com/PacktPublishing/Mastering-the-Faster-Web-with-PHP-MySQL-and-JavaScript`. In case there's an update to the code, it will be updated on the existing GitHub repository.

All the code examples given in this book can be found, within the code repository, in a folder named according to the chapter's number. Thus, it is expected that you change your working directory at the beginning of each chapter in order to run the code examples given within. Thus, for chapter 1, you are expected to enter, on the container's CLI, the following commands:

```
# mv /srv/www /srv/www.OLD
# ln -s /srv/fasterweb/chapter_1 /srv/www
```

And, for the next chapter, you are expected to enter these commands:

```
# rm /srv/www
# ln -s /srv/fasterweb/chapter_2 /srv/www
```

And, so on for the following chapters.

We also have other code bundles from our rich catalog of books and videos available at `https://github.com/PacktPublishing/`. Check them out!

Conventions used

There are a number of text conventions used throughout this book.

`CodeInText`: Indicates code words in text, database table names, folder names, filenames, file extensions, pathnames, dummy URLs, user input, and Twitter handles. Here is an example: "Whenever possible, the developer should always prefer using `const` over `let` or `var`."

A block of code is set as follows:

```
function myJS()
{
    function add(n1, n2)
    {
        let number1 = Number(n1);
        let number2 = Number(n2);

        return number1 + number2;
    }

}
```

Any command-line input or output is written as follows:

```
# php parallel-download.php
```

Bold: Indicates a new term, an important word, or words that you see onscreen. For example, words in menus or dialog boxes appear in the text like this. Here is an example: "If you scroll towards the end of the page, you should now see an **xdebug** section."

 Warnings or important notes appear like this.

 Tips and tricks appear like this.

Get in touch

Feedback from our readers is always welcome.

General feedback: Email `feedback@packtpub.com` and mention the book title in the subject of your message. If you have questions about any aspect of this book, please email us at `questions@packtpub.com`.

Errata: Although we have taken every care to ensure the accuracy of our content, mistakes do happen. If you have found a mistake in this book, we would be grateful if you would report this to us. Please visit `www.packtpub.com/submit-errata`, selecting your book, clicking on the Errata Submission Form link, and entering the details.

Piracy: If you come across any illegal copies of our works in any form on the Internet, we would be grateful if you would provide us with the location address or website name. Please contact us at copyright@packtpub.com with a link to the material.

If you are interested in becoming an author: If there is a topic that you have expertise in and you are interested in either writing or contributing to a book, please visit authors.packtpub.com.

Reviews

Please leave a review. Once you have read and used this book, why not leave a review on the site that you purchased it from? Potential readers can then see and use your unbiased opinion to make purchase decisions, we at Packt can understand what you think about our products, and our authors can see your feedback on their book. Thank you!

For more information about Packt, please visit packtpub.com.

Faster Web – Getting Started

1

The Faster Web is an expression that has been around for a few years now and has been used to designate many different aspects of web performance. In this book, we will take a closer look at what it is. Why is it important? Is it the same thing as performance? How do we measure it? When should we start thinking about it when developing a new project? What are the underlying technologies and how do we harness the power of these technologies in order to make our web projects part of the Faster Web?

In this first chapter, we will start by defining what the Faster Web is and try to better understand the formal aspects of it.

Also, throughout the entire book, we will provide many code examples that will allow us to better understand the concepts behind the Faster Web. We will take the time to look back at its origins, assess its current developments, and look forward to the future in order to understand its next important milestone.

For now, we will start with the installation of benchmarking and profiling tools inside a *Docker* container in order to learn how to use them. Also, we will take the time to understand how to measure performance and determine if a website or web application is part of the Faster Web or not.

Therefore, this chapter will cover the following points:

- Understanding what the Faster Web is and why it is important
- Learning to distinguish between the Faster Web and performance
- Knowing how to measure the Faster Web
- Installing, configuring, and using benchmark testing and profiling tools

What is the Faster Web?

In 2009, Google announced its intentions to make the web faster[1] and launched a corresponding initiative by which the web community was invited to think of ways of making the internet go faster. It was stated that *"people prefer faster, more responsive apps"* and that this was the main reason behind Google's initiative. The announcement also included a list of many challenges identified by Google as being the first order of business of this initiative. The main ones were:

- Updating aging protocols
- Fixing JavaScript's lack of performance
- Finding new measurement, diagnostics and optimization tools
- Providing more access to broadband installations across the world

The Faster Web and performance

The Faster Web can be defined as a series of qualities to be developed in all spheres of web technology in order to speed up any transaction between a client and a server.

But how important is speed? It is important enough for Google to have discovered, in 2010, that any slowdown had a direct impact on a company's website traffic and ad revenue. In fact, Google successfully established a statistical correlation between traffic and ad revenue, and the number of results and the time it takes to obtain them. The end result of their research was that it is possible to observe a decrease of the order of 20% in traffic and add revenue when obtaining more results in 0.9 seconds versus fewer results on a page in only 0.4 seconds. Yahoo also confirmed that about 5% to 9% of its users would abandon a web page that took more than 400 milliseconds to load. Microsoft Bing saw a 4% decrease in revenue when the search results were delivered with an additional delay of only 2 seconds. Clearly, speed not only ensures user engagement, but also has a major effect on a company's revenue and general performance.

At first glance, it would seem that the Faster Web is exactly the same thing as web performance. But is this really the case?

Performance is defined as the manner in which a mechanism performs. According to *André B. Bondi[2]*, *"the performance of a computer-based system is often characterized by its ability to perform defined sets of activities at fast rates and with quick response time."* And, as *J. D. Meier et al.* stated in their book on performance testing[3], *"performance testing is a type of testing intended to determine the responsiveness, throughput, reliability, and/or scalability of a system under a given workload."*

Thus, it is very clear that web performance is a core concept of the Faster Web. But, do we always expect these characteristics to be the only ones? If an application promises a thorough analysis of a hard drive and completes its task in less than five seconds, we will most certainly think that something went wrong. According to *Denys Mishunov[4]*, performance is also about perception. As stated by *Stéphanie Walter[5]* in one of her presentations on perceived performance, "*time measurement depends on the moment of measurement and can vary depending on the complexity of the task to be performed, the psychological state of the user (stress), and the user's expectations as he has defined them according to what he considers to be the software of reference when executing a certain task.*" Therefore, a good manner in which an application does what it has to do also means that the software would have to meet the user's expectations as to how this computer program ought to do things.

Even though the Faster Web initiative first concentrated its efforts on making the different web technologies go faster, the different studies led researchers back to the notion of subjective, or perceived, time versus objective, or clocked, time in order to fully measure how website performance influenced the user's habits and general behavior when it came to browsing the web.

Therefore, in this book, we will be covering the Faster Web as it applies to all the major web technologies—that is to say, those that run on 70 to 80 % of web servers around the world and on all the major browsers, namely Apache, PHP, MySQL, and JavaScript. Moreover, we will not only cover these major web technologies from a developer's standpoint, but we will also discuss the Faster Web from the system administrator's viewpoint by covering HTTP/2 and reverse proxy caching in the last chapters. And, although the greater part of this book will be addressing the question of web performance only, the last chapter will be covering the other aspect of the Faster Web, which concerns satisfying the user's expectations through good **user interface (UI)** design.

Measuring the Faster Web

Now that we better understand in what way web performance is a very important part of the Faster Web as a whole and that the Faster Web is concerned with achieving not only efficiency and speed, but also with satisfying the user's expectations entirely, we can now ask ourselves how we can objectively measure the Faster Web and which tools are best suited to do so.

Before Measuring

When discussing speed measurement, it is always important to remember that speed always ultimately depends on hardware and that poorly performing software is not necessarily a problem if it is running on a poorly performing hardware infrastructure.

Of course, **input and output** (**I/O**) always accounts for the better part of the hardware infrastructure's aggregate latency. The network and the filesystem are the two main possible bottlenecks that will offer the worst possible performance when it comes to speed. For example, accessing data on the disk can be up to a hundred times slower than **random-access memory** (**RAM**) and very busy networks can make web services practically unreachable.

RAM limits also force us to make certain tradeoffs when it comes to speed, scalability and accuracy. It is always possible to get top-speed performance by caching the greater part of an application's data and loading everything into memory. But will this be the optimal solution in all circumstances? Will it still maintain speed in the context of a heavy workload? Will the data be refreshed adequately in the context of highly volatile data? The obvious answer to these questions is probably not. Thus, optimal speed is the balance between pure speed, reasonable memory consumption and acceptable data staleness.

Measuring performance in order to determine the optimal speed of a computer program is the art of finding the perfect balance in the context of particular business rules and available resources by implementing the appropriate tradeoffs and fine-tuning them afterwards.

The first step of assessing speed performance will therefore be to analyze available resources and determine the upper and lower limits of our hardware's speed performance. And since we are working on web performance, this first step will be accomplished by benchmarking the web server itself.

The second step will consist of profiling the web application in order to analyze the performance of each part of its inner workings and determine which parts of the application's code lack perfect balance and should be optimized.

Benchmark testing and profiling

Web server benchmarking is the process of evaluating a web server's performance under a certain workload. Software profiling is the process of analyzing a computer program's use of memory and execution time in order to optimize the program's inner structure.

In this part of the chapter, we will set up and test a few of the tools that will allow us to benchmark our web server and profile the source code that we will be analyzing in the next chapters of this book.

Practical prerequisites

In order to run the source code included in this book, we recommend that you start by installing Docker on your computer (https://docs.docker.com/engine/installation/). Docker is a software container platform that allows you to easily connect to your computer's devices in an isolated and sophisticated chroot-like environment. Unlike virtual machines, containers do not come bundled with full operating systems, but rather come with the required binaries in order to run some software. You can install Docker on Windows, Mac, or Linux. It should be noted, however, that some features, like full-featured networking, are still not available when running Docker on macOS (https://docs.docker.com/docker-for-mac/networking/#known-limitations-use-cases-and-workarounds).

The main Docker image that we will be using throughout this book is *Linux for PHP* 8.1 (https://linuxforphp.net/) with a non-thread safe version of PHP 7.1.16 and *MariaDB* (*MySQL*) 10.2.8 (asclinux/linuxforphp-8.1:7.1.16-nts). Once Docker is installed on your computer, please run the following commands in a bash-like Terminal in order to get a copy of the book's code examples and start the appropriate Docker container:

```
# git clone https://github.com/andrewscaya/fasterweb
# cd fasterweb
# docker run --rm -it \
  -v ${PWD}/:/srv/fasterweb \
  -p 8181:80 \
  asclinux/linuxforphp-8.1:7.1.16-nts \
  /bin/bash
```

After running these commands, you should get the following command prompt:

The Linux for PHP container's command line interface (CLI)

Note to Windows users: please make sure to replace the '${PWD}' portion of the shared volumes option in the previous Docker command with the full path to your working directory (ex. '/c/Users/fasterweb'), because you will not be able to start the container otherwise. Also, you should make sure that volume sharing is enabled in your Docker settings. Moreover, if you are running Docker on Windows 7 or 8, you will only be able to access the container at the address http://192.168.99.100:8181 and not at 'localhost:8181'.

All the code examples given in this book can be found, within the code repository, in a folder named according to the chapter's number. Thus, it is expected that you change your working directory at the beginning of each chapter in order to run the code examples given within. Thus, for this chapter, you are expected to enter, on the container's CLI, the following commands:

```
# mv /srv/www /srv/www.OLD
# ln -s /srv/fasterweb/chapter_1 /srv/www
```

And, for the next chapter, you are expected to enter these commands:

```
# rm /srv/www
# ln -s /srv/fasterweb/chapter_2 /srv/www
```

And, so on for the following chapters.

Also, if you prefer using multithreading technologies while optimizing your code, you can do so by running the thread-safe version of *Linux for PHP* (asclinux/linuxforphp-8.1:7.0.29-zts).

If you prefer running the container in detached mode (-d switch), please do so. This will allow you to docker exec many command shells against the same container while keeping it up and running at all times independently of whether you have a running Terminal or not.

Moreover, you should docker commit any changes you made to the container and create new images of it so that you can docker run it at a later time. If you are not familiar with the Docker command line and its run command, please find the documentation at the following address: https://docs.docker.com/engine/reference/run/.

Finally, many excellent books and videos on Docker have been published by Packt Publishing and I highly recommend that you read them in order to master this fine tool.

Now, enter the following commands in order to start all the services that will be needed throughout this book and to create a test script that will allow you to make sure everything is working as expected:

```
# cd /srv/www
# /etc/init.d/mysql start
# /etc/init.d/php-fpm start
# /etc/init.d/httpd start
# touch /srv/www/index.php
# echo -e "<?php phpinfo();" > /srv/www/index.php
```

Once you are done running these commands, you should point your favorite browser to `http://localhost:8181/` and see the following result:

The phpinfo page

If you do not see this page, please try to troubleshoot your Docker installation.

Moreover, please note that, if you do not `docker commit` your changes and prefer to use an original Linux for PHP base image whenever you wish to start working with a code example contained in this book, the previous commands will have to be repeated each and every time.

We are now ready to benchmark our server.

Understanding Apache Bench (AB)

Many tools are available to benchmark a web server. The better-known ones are Apache Bench (AB), Siege, JMeter, and Tsung. Although JMeter (`https://jmeter.apache.org/`) and Tsung (`http://tsung.erlang-projects.org/`) are very interesting load-testing tools and should be explored when doing more advanced testing in the context of system administration, we will focus on AB and Siege for our development purposes.

AB is included with the Apache web server's development tools and is installed by default in Linux for PHP images that contain PHP binaries. Otherwise, AB can be found in a separate Apache development tools installation package on most Linux distributions. It is important to note that Apache Bench does not support multithreading, which can create problems when running high-concurrency tests.

Also, there are some common pitfalls to avoid when benchmarking. The main ones are:

- Avoid running other resource-hungry applications simultaneously on the computer that is being benchmarked
- Avoid benchmarking remote servers, as the network, especially in concurrency tests, might become the main cause of measured latency
- Avoid testing on web pages that are cached through HTTP accelerators or proxies, as the result will be skewed and will not reveal actual server speed performance
- Do not think that benchmarking and load testing will perfectly represent user interaction with your server, as the results are indicative in nature only
- Be aware that benchmarking results are specific to the hardware architecture being tested and will vary from one computer to the other

For our tests, we will be using *Apache Bench*'s −k, −1, −c, and −n switches. Here are the definitions of these switches:

- −k enables the KeepAlive feature in order to perform multiple requests in one single HTTP session
- −1 disables error reporting when the content lengths vary in size from one response to the other
- −c enables concurrency in order to perform multiple requests at the same time
- −n determines the number of requests to perform in the current benchmarking session

For more information on AB's options, please see the corresponding entry in *Apache*'s documentation (https://httpd.apache.org/docs/2.4/programs/ab.html).

Before launching the benchmark tests, open a new Terminal window and docker exec a new bash Terminal to the container. This way, you will be able to see resource consumption through the top utility. To do so, start by getting the name of your container. It will appear in the list that will be returned by this command:

```
# docker ps
```

You will then be able to tap into the container and start watching resource consumption with the following command:

```
# docker exec −it [name_of_your_container_here] /bin/bash
```

And, on the container's newly obtained command line, please run the top command:

```
# top
```

Now, launch a benchmark test from within the first Terminal window:

```
# ab −k −1 −c 2 −n 2000 localhost/index.html
```

You will then get a benchmark test report containing information on the average number of requests per second that the server was able to respond to (Requests per second), the average response time per request (Time per request) and the response time's standard deviation (Percentage of requests served within a certain time (ms)).

The report should be similar to the following:

```
andrewdevmac — docker run --rm -it -v ~/:/srv/www -p 8181:80 asclinux/mast...
root@e5523bd5037c [ / ]# ab -k -l -c 2 -n 2000 localhost/index.html
This is ApacheBench, Version 2.3 <$Revision: 1748469 $>
Copyright 1996 Adam Twiss, Zeus Technology Ltd, http://www.zeustech.net/
Licensed to The Apache Software Foundation, http://www.apache.org/

Benchmarking localhost (be patient)
Completed 200 requests
Completed 400 requests
Completed 600 requests
Completed 800 requests
Completed 1000 requests
Completed 1200 requests
Completed 1400 requests
Completed 1600 requests
Completed 1800 requests
Completed 2000 requests
Finished 2000 requests


Server Software:        Apache/2.4.23
Server Hostname:        localhost
Server Port:            80

Document Path:          /index.html
Document Length:        Variable

Concurrency Level:      2
Time taken for tests:   2.448 seconds
Complete requests:      2000
Failed requests:        0
Keep-Alive requests:    1982
Total transferred:      583209 bytes
HTML transferred:       26000 bytes
Requests per second:    816.89  [#/sec] (mean)
Time per request:       2.448 [ms] (mean)
Time per request:       1.224 [ms] (mean, across all concurrent requests)
Transfer rate:          232.63 [Kbytes/sec] received

Connection Times (ms)
              min  mean[+/-sd] median   max
Connect:        0    0   0.0      0       0
Processing:     2    2   0.4      2       8
Waiting:        1    2   0.4      2       8
Total:          2    2   0.4      2       8

Percentage of the requests served within a certain time (ms)
  50%      2
  66%      3
  75%      3
  80%      3
  90%      3
  95%      3
  98%      3
  99%      4
 100%      8 (longest request)
root@e5523bd5037c [ / ]#
```

The benchmark report shows that Apache is serving about 817 requests per second on average

Now, try a new benchmark test by requesting the index.php file:

```
# ab -k -l -c 2 -n 2000 localhost/index.php
```

You will notice that the average number of requests per second has dropped and that the average response time and the standard deviation are higher. In my case, the average has dropped from about 800 to around 300 on my computer, the average response time has passed from 2 milliseconds to 6 milliseconds and the response time's standard deviation has now gone from 100% of requests being served within 8 milliseconds to 24 milliseconds:

```
●  ○  ◎  ⌂  andrewdevmac — docker run --rm -it -v ~/:/srv/www -p 8181:80 asclinux/mast...
root@e5523bd5037c [ / ]# ab -k -l -c 2 -n 2000 localhost/index.php
This is ApacheBench, Version 2.3 <$Revision: 1748469 $>
Copyright 1996 Adam Twiss, Zeus Technology Ltd, http://www.zeustech.net/
Licensed to The Apache Software Foundation, http://www.apache.org/

Benchmarking localhost (be patient)
Completed 200 requests
Completed 400 requests
Completed 600 requests
Completed 800 requests
Completed 1000 requests
Completed 1200 requests
Completed 1400 requests
Completed 1600 requests
Completed 1800 requests
Completed 2000 requests
Finished 2000 requests


Server Software:        Apache/2.4.23
Server Hostname:        localhost
Server Port:            80

Document Path:          /index.php
Document Length:        Variable

Concurrency Level:      2
Time taken for tests:   6.387 seconds
Complete requests:      2000
Failed requests:        0
Keep-Alive requests:    0
Total transferred:      139103788 bytes
HTML transferred:       138763788 bytes
Requests per second:    313.13 [#/sec] (mean)
Time per request:       6.387 [ms] (mean)
Time per request:       3.194 [ms] (mean, across all concurrent requests)
Transfer rate:          21268.19 [Kbytes/sec] received

Connection Times (ms)
              min  mean[+/-sd] median   max
Connect:        0    0   0.0      0       1
Processing:     4    6   1.2      6      23
Waiting:        4    6   1.1      6      23
Total:          4    6   1.2      6      24

Percentage of the requests served within a certain time (ms)
  50%      6
  66%      6
  75%      7
  80%      7
  90%      7
  95%      8
  98%      9
  99%     10
 100%     24 (longest request)
root@e5523bd5037c [ / ]# ▮
```

The benchmark report shows that Apache is now serving about 313 requests per second on average

These results allow us to have a general idea of our hardware's performance limits and to determine the different thresholds we would have to deal with when scaling performance of PHP scripts that are generating some dynamic content.

Now, let's dig a little deeper into our web server's performance with Siege, a tool of choice when benchmarking and load testing.

Understanding Siege

Siege is a load testing and benchmarking tool that allows us to further analyze our web server's performance. Let's begin by installing Siege inside our Docker container.

From the container's command line, please download and decompress version 4.0.2 of Siege:

```
# wget -O siege-4.0.2.tar.gz
http://download.joedog.org/siege/siege-4.0.2.tar.gz
# tar -xzvf siege-4.0.2.tar.gz
```

Then, please enter Siege's source code directory to compile and install the software:

```
# cd siege-4.0.2
# ./configure
# make
# make install
```

For these tests with Siege, we will be using the -b, -c, and -r switches. Here are the definitions of these switches:

- -b, enables benchmark mode, which means that there are no delays between iterations
- -c, enables concurrency in order to perform multiple requests at the same time
- -r, determines the number of requests to perform with each concurrent user

Of course, you can get more information on Siege's command-line options by invoking the manual from the container's command line:

```
# man siege
```

Now launch a Siege benchmark test:

```
# siege -b -c 3000 -r 100 localhost/index.html
```

You will then get a benchmark test report like this one:

```
●  ◉  ◉   ⌂ andrewdevmac — docker run --rm -it -v ~/:/srv/www -p 8181:80 asclinux/mast...
HTTP/1.1 200     0.01 secs:      13 bytes ==> GET  /index.html
HTTP/1.1 200     0.01 secs:      13 bytes ==> GET  /index.html
HTTP/1.1 200     0.00 secs:      13 bytes ==> GET  /index.html
HTTP/1.1 200     0.00 secs:      13 bytes ==> GET  /index.html
HTTP/1.1 200     0.00 secs:      13 bytes ==> GET  /index.html
HTTP/1.1 200     0.01 secs:      13 bytes ==> GET  /index.html
HTTP/1.1 200     0.00 secs:      13 bytes ==> GET  /index.html
HTTP/1.1 200     0.00 secs:      13 bytes ==> GET  /index.html
HTTP/1.1 200     0.00 secs:      13 bytes ==> GET  /index.html

Transactions:                25500 hits
Availability:                100.00 %
Elapsed time:                 32.13 secs
Data transferred:              0.32 MB
Response time:                 0.25 secs
Transaction rate:            793.65 trans/sec
Throughput:                    0.01 MB/sec
Concurrency:                 195.77
Successful transactions:     25500
Failed transactions:             0
Longest transaction:          3.51
Shortest transaction:         0.00

root@f34438580750 [ / ]#
```

The Siege benchmark report confirms the results that were obtained from AB

As you can see, the results match those that we got from AB previously. Our test shows a transaction rate of almost 800 transactions per second.

Siege also comes with a handy tool named Bombard that can automate tests and help to verify scalability. Bombard allows you to use Siege with an ever-increasing number of concurrent users. It can take a few optional arguments. These are: the name of a file containing URLs to use when performing the tests, the number of initial concurrent clients, the number of concurrent clients to add each time Siege is called, the number of times Bombard should call Siege and the time delay, in seconds, between each request.

We can, therefore, try to confirm the results of our previous tests by issuing the following commands inside the container:

```
# cd /srv/www
# touch urlfile.txt
# for i in {1..4}; do echo "http://localhost/index.html" >> urlfile.txt ;
done
# bombardment urlfile.txt 10 100 4 0
```

Once done, you should obtain a report similar to the following one:

```
andrewdevmac — docker run --rm -it -v ~/:/srv/www -p 8181:80 asclinux/mast...
** SIEGE 4.0.2
** Preparing 110 concurrent users for battle.
The server is now under siege...

Lifting the server siege...
Transactions:                 362727 hits
Availability:                 100.00 %
Elapsed time:                 300.02 secs
Data transferred:               4.50 MB
Response time:                  0.09 secs
Transaction rate:            1209.01 trans/sec
Throughput:                     0.01 MB/sec
Concurrency:                  104.14
Successful transactions:      362727
Failed transactions:               0
Longest transaction:            0.69
Shortest transaction:           0.00

Starting run number 3
** SIEGE 4.0.2
** Preparing 210 concurrent users for battle.
The server is now under siege...

Lifting the server siege...
Transactions:                 360510 hits
Availability:                 100.00 %
Elapsed time:                 300.03 secs
Data transferred:               4.47 MB
Response time:                  0.17 secs
Transaction rate:            1201.58 trans/sec
Throughput:                     0.01 MB/sec
Concurrency:                  200.54
Successful transactions:      360513
Failed transactions:               0
Longest transaction:            7.36
Shortest transaction:           0.00

Starting run number 4
** SIEGE 4.0.2
** Preparing 255 concurrent users for battle.
The server is now under siege...

Lifting the server siege...
Transactions:                 358487 hits
Availability:                 100.00 %
Elapsed time:                 299.91 secs
Data transferred:               4.44 MB
Response time:                  0.21 secs
Transaction rate:            1195.32 trans/sec
Throughput:                     0.01 MB/sec
Concurrency:                  245.22
Successful transactions:      358487
Failed transactions:               0
Longest transaction:            7.41
Shortest transaction:           0.00
```

The results show that the longest transaction is much higher when there are 210 or more concurrent users

Try again, but by requesting the PHP file:

```
# echo "http://localhost/index.php" > urlfile.txt
# for i in {1..3}; do echo "http://localhost/index.php" >> urlfile.txt ;
done
# bombardment urlfile.txt 10 100 4 0
```

This test should provide results similar to these:

```
andrewdevmac — docker run --rm -it -v ~/:/srv/www -p 8181:80 asclinux/mast...
** Preparing 110 concurrent users for battle.
The server is now under siege...

Lifting the server siege...
Transactions:                   44430 hits
Availability:                  100.00 %
Elapsed time:                  239.98 secs
Data transferred:             2945.00 MB
Response time:                   0.59 secs
Transaction rate:              185.14 trans/sec
Throughput:                     12.27 MB/sec
Concurrency:                   109.04
Successful transactions:        44430
Failed transactions:                0
Longest transaction:             0.87
Shortest transaction:            0.10

Starting run number 3
** SIEGE 4.0.2
** Preparing 210 concurrent users for battle.
The server is now under siege...

Lifting the server siege...
Transactions:                   41747 hits
Availability:                   99.95 %
Elapsed time:                  239.93 secs
Data transferred:             2767.17 MB
Response time:                   1.20 secs
Transaction rate:              174.00 trans/sec
Throughput:                     11.53 MB/sec
Concurrency:                   207.97
Successful transactions:        41747
Failed transactions:               19
Longest transaction:            61.21
Shortest transaction:            0.24

Starting run number 4
** SIEGE 4.0.2
** Preparing 255 concurrent users for battle.
The server is now under siege...

Lifting the server siege...
Transactions:                   39193 hits
Availability:                   99.78 %
Elapsed time:                  239.92 secs
Data transferred:             2597.90 MB
Response time:                   1.54 secs
Transaction rate:              163.36 trans/sec
Throughput:                     10.83 MB/sec
Concurrency:                   252.26
Successful transactions:        39193
Failed transactions:               86
Longest transaction:            63.22
Shortest transaction:            0.13

root@f3443858075Q [ / ]#
```

The efficiency of serving dynamic content is analogous to that of serving static content, but with a much lower transaction rate

The second Terminal window that is running `top` is now showing 50% usage of both of the available processors and almost 50% RAM usage on my computer:

The container's usage of CPU and memory resources when it is submitted to benchmarking tests

We now know that, when there are not many concurrent requests, this hardware can allow for good performance on a small scale, with 800 transactions per second on static files and about 200 transactions per second on pages that have dynamically generated content.

Now that we have a better idea of the base speed performance of our web server based solely on our hardware's resources, we can now start to truly measure the speed and efficiency of the web server's dynamically generated content through profiling. We will now proceed to install and configure tools that will allow us to profile and optimize PHP code.

Installing and configuring useful tools

We will now install and configure MySQL benchmarking and JavaScript profiling tools. But first, let's start by installing and configuring xdebug, a PHP debugger and profiler.

Profiling PHP – xdebug Installation and Configuration

The first tool we will install and configure is xdebug, a debugging and profiling tool for PHP. This extension can be downloaded, decompressed, configured, compiled and installed in a very easy manner by using the PECL utility included with PHP (https://pecl.php.net/). To do this, inside the container's Terminal window, please enter the following commands:

```
# pecl install xdebug
# echo -e "zend_extension=$( php -i | grep extensions | awk '{print $3}' )/xdebug.so\n" >> /etc/php.ini
# echo -e "xdebug.remote_enable = 1\n" >> /etc/php.ini
# echo -e "xdebug.remote_enable_trigger = 1\n" >> /etc/php.ini
# echo -e "xdebug.remote_connect_back = 1\n" >> /etc/php.ini
# echo -e "xdebug.idekey = PHPSTORM\n" >> /etc/php.ini
# echo -e "xdebug.profiler_enable = 1\n" >> /etc/php.ini
# echo -e "xdebug.profiler_enable_trigger = 1\n" >> /etc/php.ini
# /etc/init.d/php-fpm restart
# tail -50 /etc/php.ini
```

The last lines of your container's /etc/php.ini file should now look like this:

Newly added lines to the php.ini file

Once done, please reload the `http://localhost:8181` page in your favorite browser. It should now read as follows:

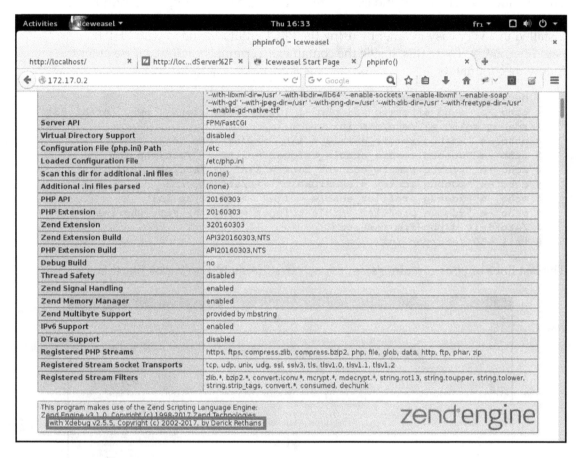

Confirmation that the xdebug extension has been loaded

If you scroll towards the end of the page, you should now see an **xdebug** section:

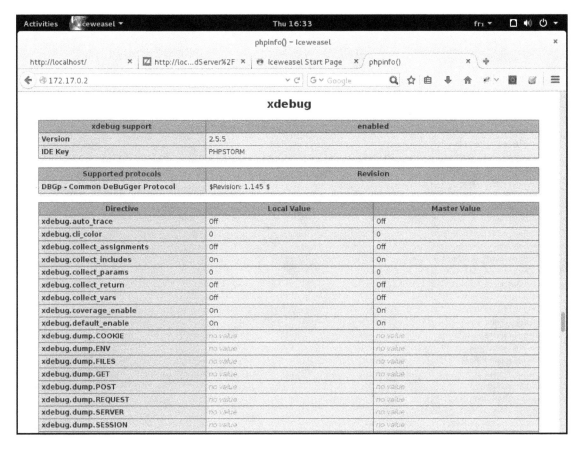

The xdebug section of the phpinfo page

You should also notice that the profiler options are now enabled under the xdebug entry:

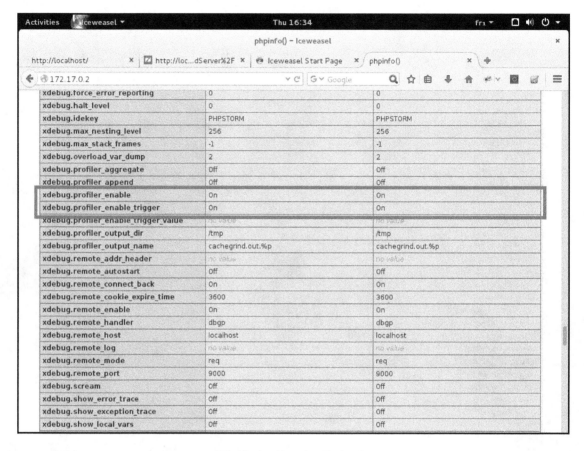

Confirmation that xdebug code profiling is enabled

We will now configure PHPStorm to be the debugging server. This will allow us to use our IDE as the control center for our debugging sessions.

Before we start, we will make the entire `fasterweb` folder available as the server's web root directory by entering these commands inside the container:

```
# rm /srv/www
# ln -s /srv/fasterweb /srv/www
# cd /srv/www
```

Now, start *PHPStorm* and make our `fasterweb` directory the home root of this project. To do so, select **Create New Project from Existing Files** and **Source files are in a local directory** and designate our `fasterweb` directory as the **Project root** before clicking on **Finish**.

Once created, select **Settings** from within the **File** menu. Under the **Languages & Frameworks** section, unfold the **PHP** menu entry and click on the **Servers** entry. Please enter all the appropriate information according to the specifics of your setup. The **Host** option must contain the value of the IP address of the Linux for PHP container. If you are not sure what is the IP address of your Docker container, please enter the following command on the container's command line in order to obtain it:

```
# ifconfig
```

Once done, you can confirm by clicking on the **Apply** and **OK** buttons:

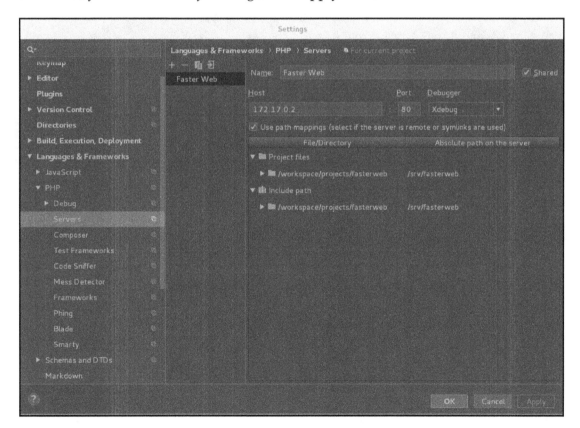

Configuring PHPStorm to connect to the web server and xdebug

Then, under the **Run** menu, you will find the **Edit Configurations...** entry. It can also be found on the right-hand side of the IDE's screen:

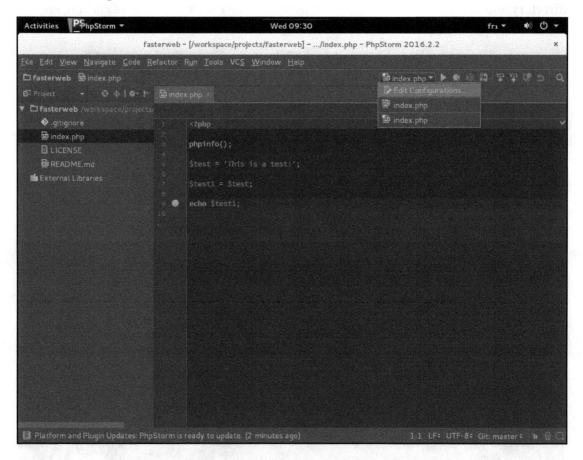

The 'Edit configurations...' setting

You can then add a **PHP Remote Debug** entry by clicking on the green plus sign in the upper-left corner of this window. Please select the server that we created in the previous step and please make sure that the **Ide key(session id)** is set to **PHPSTORM**:

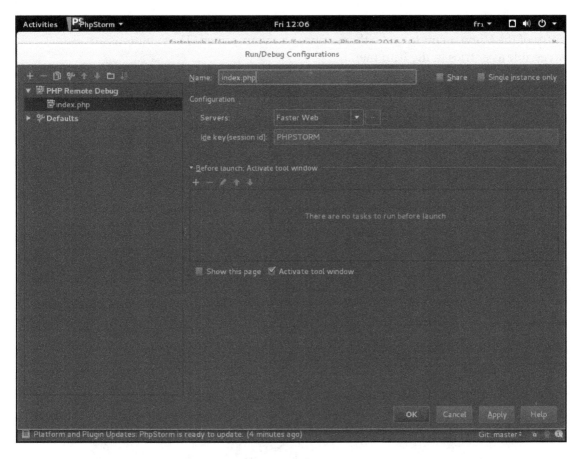

Configuring the debugging session

You can now activate the PHPStorm debugging server by clicking on the **Listen to debugger connections** button in the upper-right menu of the main PHPStorm screen, set a breakpoint by clicking in the space to the right of any line number of the index.php file, and launch the debug tool corresponding to the index.php configuration that we created in the previous step.

If the top-right toolbar menu is not displayed on your screen, please click on the **Toolbar** entry of the **View** menu to make them appear on your screen. These buttons are also accessible as entries in the **Run** menu.

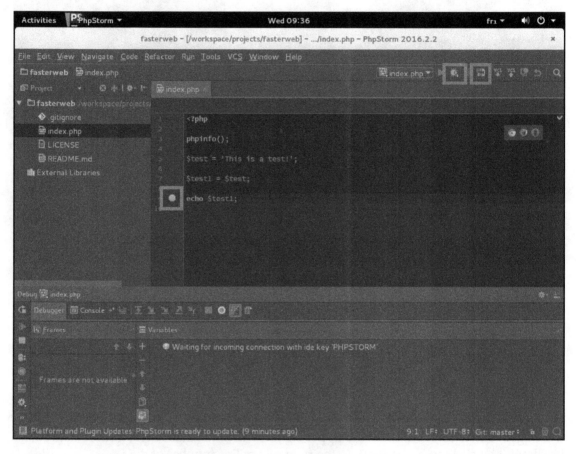

Activating the PHPStorm debugging server, setting a breakpoint and launching the debug tool

Now, open your favorite browser and request the same web page by entering the IP address of your Docker container:
`http://[IP_ADDRESS]/?XDEBUG_SESSION_START=PHPSTORM`.

You will then notice that the browser is caught in an infinite loop:

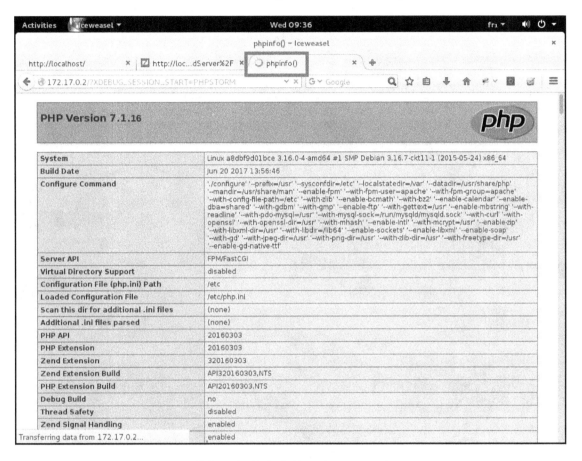

The browser is waiting for the debug session to resume or end

You will also notice that the debugging information is now showing inside the IDE. We can also control the session and determine when execution will resume from within the IDE. Please inspect the contents of the variables before allowing execution to resume by clicking on the green play button on the left-hand side of the screen. You can also end the debugging session by clicking on the pink stop button in the same icon menu:

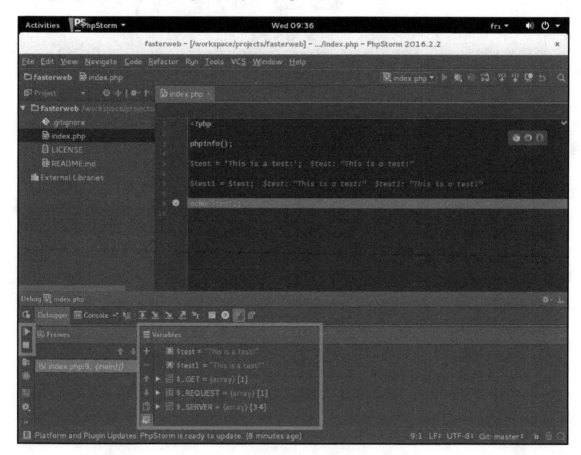

The debugging session allows for detailed inspection of variables during runtime

Once the debugging session is over, we can now inspect our container's /tmp directory and should find the profiler output in a file named cachegrind.out. You can then inspect this file directly through your favorite text editor or by installing specialized software such as Kcachegrind with the package manager of your Linux distribution. Here is a sample output when using Kcachegrind:

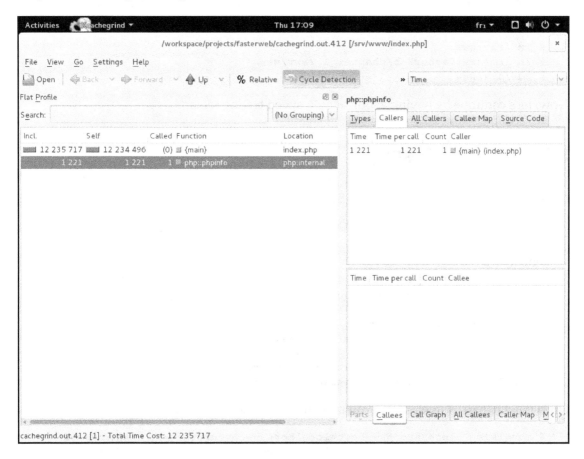

Viewing the xdebug profiling report with Kcachegrind

Thus, xdebug's profiling tool will be available to you if you wish to use it on top of those that we will be using to optimize our code examples in the next chapters. This being said, in the next chapter, we will be looking into more advanced profiling tools such as `Blackfire.io`.

Once you are done testing xdebug, you can restore the `chapter_1` folder as the server's web root directory:

```
# rm /srv/www
# ln -s /srv/fasterweb/chapter_1 /srv/www
# cd /srv/www
```

Now, let's continue by having a look at SQL speed testing tools.

SQL – Speed Testing

Even though the PostgreSQL server is often considered to be the fastest RDBMS in the world after *Oracle Database*, the *MariaDB* (fork of *MySQL*) server remains one of the fastest and most popular RDBMSs, especially when it comes to simple SQL queries. Thus, when discussing SQL optimizations in this book, we will mostly use *MariaDB*.

To benchmark our *MariaDB* server, we will be using the `mysqlslap` utility included with *MySQL* servers since version 5.1.4. In order to run the tests, we will start by loading the `Sakila` test database. On the container's command line, enter the following commands:

```
# wget -O sakila-db.tar.gz \
> https://downloads.mysql.com/docs/sakila-db.tar.gz
# tar -xzvf sakila-db.tar.gz
# mysql -uroot < sakila-db/sakila-schema.sql
# mysql -uroot < sakila-db/sakila-data.sql
```

Once the database is loaded, you can launch the first benchmarking test:

```
# mysqlslap --user=root --host=localhost --concurrency=20 --number-of-
queries=1000 --create-schema=sakila --query="SELECT * FROM film;" --
delimiter=";" --verbose --iterations=2 --debug-info
```

You should then obtain a result similar to this:

Benchmarking the MariaDB server with the mysqlslap tool

You can then run a second benchmark test, but with a different level of concurrency in order to compare the results:

```
# mysqlslap --user=root --host=localhost --concurrency=50 --number-of-
queries=1000 --create-schema=sakila --query="SELECT * FROM film;" --
delimiter=";" --verbose --iterations=2 --debug-info
```

Here are the results of the second test:

Benchmarking the MariaDB server with the mysqlslap tool using higher concurrency

The results of my tests show me that, with a full table scan query on a table with approximately 1,000 entries, performance degrades drastically when 50 or more concurrent queries are sent to the server.

We will see how these types of tests and many other more advanced ones will be particularly useful when discussing SQL query optimizations in the chapters dedicated to this topic.

JavaScript – Developer Tools

In order to measure performance and profile the JavaScript code contained in this book, we will use Google Chrome's built-in developer tools. Specifically, Chrome includes a timeline recorder and JavaScript CPU profiler that will allow you to identify bottlenecks in your JavaScript code. To activate these tools, please click on the three dots in the upper-right corner of the browser and click on the **Developer Tools** entry in the **More Tools** submenu, as shown:

Finding the 'Developer Tools' entry in the 'More Tools' section of Chrome's main menu

Using the profiler is as easy as clicking the **Record** button and refreshing the page you wish to profile. You can then analyze the results in order to identify potential problems with the code:

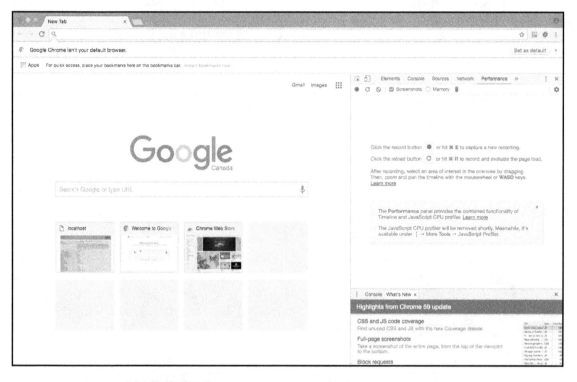

Chrome's timeline recorder and JavaScript CPU profiler

In Chapter 7, *JavaScript and "Danger Driven Development"*, and Chapter 8, *Functional JavaScript*, we will be using this tool more extensively in order to measure and optimize JavaScript code performance in general.

Summary

In this chapter, we have defined what the Faster Web is, why it is important, how it distinguishes itself from pure speed performance and how to install, configure and use benchmark testing and profiling tools in order to measure it.

In the next chapter, we will discover automatic profiling with `Blackfire.io`. Also, we will learn about monitoring by installing and configuring a TICK stack with Grafana on a fictitious production server that will be deployed as another Docker container.

References

[1] https://googleblog.blogspot.ca/2009/06/lets-make-web-faster.html

[2] *BONDI, André B. Foundations of Software and System Performance Engineering: Process, Performance Modeling, Requirements, Testing, Scalability, and Practice. Upper Saddle River, NJ: Addison-Wesley, 2015.*

[3] *MEIER, J. D. et al. Performance Testing Guidance for Web Applications. Redmond, WA: Microsoft Corporation, 2007.*

[4] https://www.smashingmagazine.com/2015/11/why-performance-matters-part-2-perception-management/

[5] https://speakerd.s3.amazonaws.com/presentations/2ece664392024e9da39ea82e3d9f1139/perception-performance-ux-confoo-3-4.pdf

2
Continuous Profiling and Monitoring

In this chapter, we will learn how to install and configure profiling and monitoring tools that will help you easily optimize PHP code in a **continuous integration** (**CI**) and a **continuous deployment** (**CD**) environment.

We will start by installing and configuring a basic `Blackfire.io` setup in order to easily and automatically profile code when committing it to a repository. We will also learn how to install a TICK Stack in order to continuously monitor our code's performance after its deployment on a live production server.

Thus, in this chapter, we will cover the following points:

- Installing and configuring the `Blackfire.io` agent, client and PHP extension
- Integrating the `Blackfire.io` client with Google Chrome
- Integrating the `Blackfire.io` client with a known CI tool like Travis
- Installing and configuring a complete TICK Stack with Grafana

What is Blackfire.io?

As stated on the official Blackfire website (`https://blackfire.io`), *Blackfire empowers all developers and IT/Ops to continuously verify and improve their app's performance, throughout its life cycle, by getting the right information at the right moment. It is, therefore, a performance management solution that allows you to automatically profile your code and set performance standards through assertions throughout your application's life cycle, especially in the development phase.* `Blackfire.io` is a tool that makes what Fabien Potencier calls *performance as a feature* possible, by making performance tests a part of the development cycle from the very beginning of a project.

Installing and configuring Blackfire.io

Installing and configuring `Blackfire.io` means setting up three components: the agent, the client and the PHP Probe. In the context of this book, we will be installing `Blackfire.io` inside our Linux for PHP container. To get more information on installing `Blackfire.io` on another operating system, please see the following instructions: `https://blackfire.io/docs/up-and-running/installation`.

We will start by installing the Blackfire agent. On the container's command-line interface, enter the following commands:

```
# rm /srv/www
# ln -s /srv/fasterweb/chapter_2 /srv/www
# cd /srv/www
# wget -O blackfire-agent
https://packages.blackfire.io/binaries/blackfire-agent/1.17.0/blackfire-agent-linux_static_amd64
```

Once the download is completed, you should see the following result:

Blackfire agent download is done

If so, please continue by typing these commands:

```
# mv blackfire-agent /usr/local/bin/
# chmod +x /usr/local/bin/blackfire-agent
```

Now, we will copy a basic agent configuration file to our etc directory:

```
# mkdir -p /etc/blackfire
# cp agent /etc/blackfire/
```

Here is the content of the file we just copied. It is a basic configuration file, as suggested by the Blackfire team:

```
[blackfire]
;
; setting: ca-cert
; desc    : Sets the PEM encoded certificates
; default:
ca-cert=

;
; setting: collector
; desc    : Sets the URL of Blackfire's data collector
; default: https://blackfire.io
collector=https://blackfire.io/

;
; setting: log-file
; desc    : Sets the path of the log file. Use stderr to log to stderr
; default: stderr
log-file=stderr

;
; setting: log-level
; desc    : log verbosity level (4: debug, 3: info, 2: warning, 1: error)
; default: 1
log-level=1

;
; setting: server-id
; desc    : Sets the server id used to authenticate with Blackfire API
; default:
server-id=

;
; setting: server-token
; desc    : Sets the server token used to authenticate with Blackfire
API. It is unsafe to set this from the command line
```

```
; default:
server-token=


;
; setting: socket
; desc    : Sets the socket the agent should read traces from. Possible
value can be a unix socket or a TCP address
; default: unix:///var/run/blackfire/agent.sock on Linux,
unix:///usr/local/var/run/blackfire-agent.sock on MacOSX, and
tcp://127.0.0.1:8307 on Windows.
socket=unix:///var/run/blackfire/agent.sock


;
; setting: spec
; desc    : Sets the path to the json specifications file
; default:
spec=
```

Then, create an empty file that will be used as the agent's socket:

```
# mkdir -p /var/run/blackfire
# touch /var/run/blackfire/agent.sock
```

Finally, we will register our agent with the Blackfire service:

```
# blackfire-agent -register
```

Once you will have entered the last command, you will have to supply your Blackfire server credentials. These can be found in your Blackfire account at: https://blackfire.io/ account#server. Once you have entered your credentials, you can start the agent by entering the following command:

```
# blackfire-agent start &
```

After starting the agent, you should see the agent's PID number. This tells you that the agent is listening on the default UNIX socket that we created previously. In this example, the agent has a PID number of eight (8):

Blackfire agent process ID number is displayed

Once the agent is installed and configured, you can install the Blackfire client. We will install and configure the client by issuing the following commands. Let's start by downloading the binary:

```
# wget -O blackfire
https://packages.blackfire.io/binaries/blackfire-agent/1.17.0/blackfire-cli
-linux_static_amd64
```

After the download is done, you should see the following message:

Blackfire client download is done

You can now proceed to configure the client. Enter the following commands:

```
# mv blackfire /usr/local/bin/
# chmod +x /usr/local/bin/blackfire
# blackfire config
```

After entering the final command, you will have to supply your Blackfire client credentials. These can also be found in your Blackfire account at the following URL: `https://blackfire.io/account#client`.

The final step in order to run `Blackfire.io` on our server is to install the Blackfire Probe as a PHP extension. In order to do this, please start by downloading the library:

```
# wget -O blackfire.so
https://packages.blackfire.io/binaries/blackfire-php/1.20.0/blackfire-php-l
inux_amd64-php-71.so
```

Once the download is completed, you should get this confirmation message:

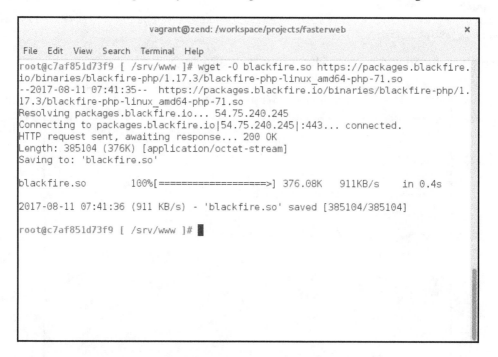

Blackfire probe download is done

You can then copy the shared library file into your PHP extensions directory. If you are not sure of this directory's location, you can issue the following command before moving the library file into it:

```
# php -i | grep 'extension_dir'
# mv blackfire.so $( php -i | grep extensions | awk '{print $3}' )
```

In this example, the extension's directory is /usr/lib/php/extensions/no-debug-non-zts-20160303.

You can now configure the extension in the PHP.INI file. When activating the Blackfire Probe, it is recommended that you deactivate other debugging and profiling extensions such as xdebug. Please run the following commands (alternatively, you can copy and paste the PHP.INI file that is included in our repository and already contains these modifications):

```
# sed -i 's/zend_extension=\/usr\/lib\/php\/extensions\/no-debug-non-
zts-20160303\/xdebug.so/;zend_extension=\/usr\/lib\/php\/extensions\/no-
debug-non-zts-20160303\/xdebug.so/' /etc/php.ini
# sed -i 's/^xdebug/;xdebug/' /etc/php.ini
# cat >>/etc/php.ini << 'EOF'

[blackfire]
extension=blackfire.so
; On Windows use the following configuration:
; extension=php_blackfire.dll

; Sets the socket where the agent is listening.
; Possible value can be a unix socket or a TCP address.
; Defaults to unix:///var/run/blackfire/agent.sock on Linux,
; unix:///usr/local/var/run/blackfire-agent.sock on MacOSX,
; and to tcp://127.0.0.1:8307 on Windows.
;blackfire.agent_socket = unix:///var/run/blackfire/agent.sock

blackfire.agent_timeout = 0.25

; Log verbosity level (4: debug, 3: info, 2: warning, 1: error)
;blackfire.log_level = 1

; Log file (STDERR by default)
;blackfire.log_file = /tmp/blackfire.log

;blackfire.server_id =

;blackfire.server_token =
EOF
```

Please complete the extension's installation and configuration by restarting PHP-FPM:

```
# /etc/init.d/php-fpm restart
```

Let's profile our first script from the command line. You can now run the client by entering the following command on the container's CLI:

```
# blackfire curl http://localhost/index.php
```

Once the profile is completed, you will obtain a URL and some profile statistics. If you browse to the URL, you will see the profile's call graph and get more detailed information on the profiled script:

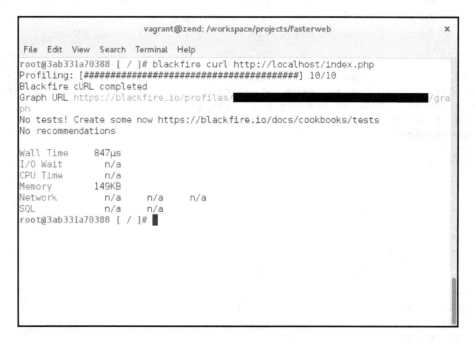

The Blackfire client returns a preliminary profiling report and a URL to view the script's call graph

You also have the option of installing the client as a browser plugin. In this example, we will be using the Blackfire Companion, a Google Chrome extension. To install the extension, visit the following URL with Chrome and click on the install button: `https://blackfire.io/docs/integrations/chrome`. Once done, it will be possible to profile the resources on the server by browsing to the page and clicking on the Blackfire Companion's icon in the toolbar and then, on the **Profile** button:

Blackfire Companion for Chrome allows you to profile a PHP script directly from the browser

Profiling manually with Blackfire.io

We will start by profiling manually two PHP scripts in order to better understand how useful and powerful the Blackfire tools can be. We will use the following script, which can be found in our repository (chap2pre.php):

```php
<?php

function getDiskUsage(string $directory)
{
    $handle = popen("cd $directory && du -ch --exclude='./.*'", 'r');

    $du = stream_get_contents($handle);
```

```php
    pclose($handle);

    return $du;
}

function getDirList(string $directory, string &$du)
{
    $result = getDiskUsage($directory);

    $du = empty($du)
        ? '<br />' . preg_replace('/\n+/', '<br />', $result)
        : $du;

    $fileList = [];

    $iterator = new RecursiveDirectoryIterator($directory,
FilesystemIterator::SKIP_DOTS);

    foreach($iterator as $entry) {

        if (!$entry->isDir() && $entry->getFilename()[0] != '.') {
            $fileList[$entry->getFilename()] = 'size is ' .
$entry->getSize();
        } else {
            if ($entry->isDir() && $entry->getFilename()[0] != '.') {
                $fileList[$entry->getFilename()] = getDirList(
                    $directory . DIRECTORY_SEPARATOR .
$entry->getFilename(),
                    $du
                );
    }
        }

    }

    return $fileList;
}

$du = '';

$baseDirectory = dirname(__FILE__);

$fileList = getDirList($baseDirectory, $du);

echo '<html><head></head><body><p>';

echo 'Disk Usage : ' . $du . '<br /><br /><br />';
```

```
echo 'Directory Name : ' . $baseDirectory . '<br /><br />';

echo 'File listing :';

echo '</p><pre>';

print_r($fileList);

echo '</pre></body></html>';
```

The script essentially lists all files contained in our repository (the directory and its subdirectories) and calculates the size of each file. Also, it gives an aggregate result of the sizes of each directory. Please browse to the following URL with Chrome to see the script's output and launch a profile using the Blackfire Companion:
`http://localhost:8181/chap2pre.php`:

Clicking on the Blackfire icon in the upper-right toolbar will allow you to launch a profiling session

After clicking on the **Profile** button and waiting a few seconds, you should then have the option of clicking the **View Call Graph** button:

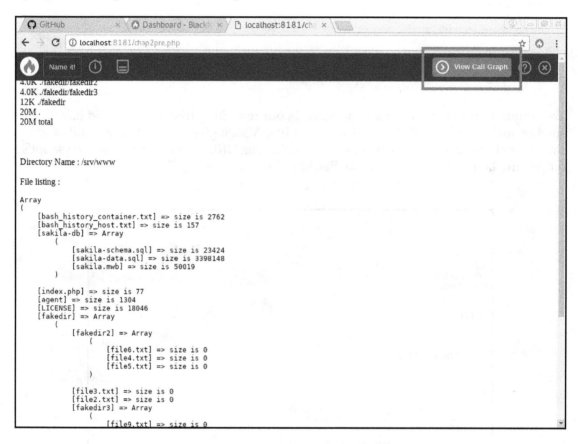

You can click on the 'View call graph' button to view the script's call graph

The results should be as follows:

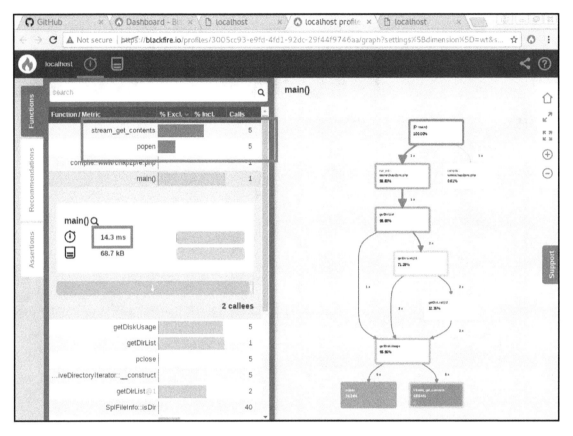

The script took 14.3 ms to complete its execution and five processes were created using the 'popen' function

The result shows us that this script has a real time (wall time[1]) of 14.3 ms and that the only functions with important exclusive times are `stream_get_contents` and `popen`. This is logical, as the script has to deal with disk access and possibly a lot of I/O latency. What is less logical is that the script seems to be creating five sub-processes in order to get a simple file listing.

Also, if we scroll down, we notice that `SplInfo::getFilename` is called sixty-seven times, which is almost twice the number of files in the directory:

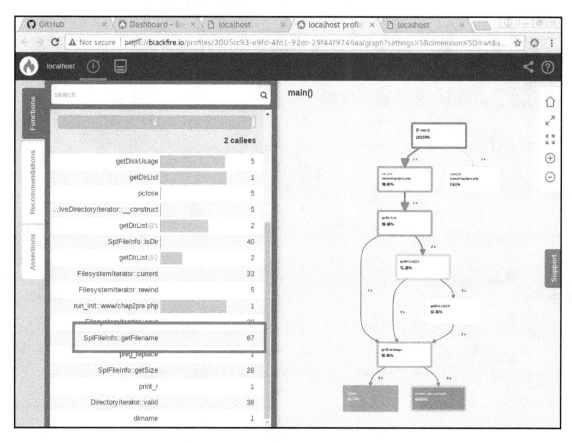

The SplFileInfo::getFilename function was called 67 times

The information obtained from the profiler allows us to quickly identify which parts of our code base should become code review candidates and what to look for when reviewing them. A quick look at our code shows us that we are calling `popen` on every directory iteration, rather than only once at the beginning. A simple fix would be to replace these two lines of code:

```
function getDirList(string $directory, string &$du)
{
    $result = getDiskUsage($directory);

    $du = empty($du)
        ? '<br />' . preg_replace('/\n+/', '<br />', $result)
```

```
        : $du;
[...]
```

The following lines of code could then be inserted in their place:

```php
function getDirList(string $directory, string &$du)
{
    $du = empty($du)
        ? '<br />' . preg_replace('/\n+/', '<br />',
getDiskUsage($directory))
        : $du;

[...]
```

The final adjustment would be to replace all calls to `SplInfo::getFilename()` with a variable containing the result of the function call. The modified script would then look as follows:

```php
<?php

function getDiskUsage(string $directory)
{
    $handle = popen("cd $directory && du -ch --exclude='./.*'", 'r');

    $du = stream_get_contents($handle);

    pclose($handle);

    return $du;
}

function getDirList(string $directory, string &$du)
{
    $du = empty($du)
        ? '<br />' . preg_replace('/\n+/', '<br />',
getDiskUsage($directory))
        : $du;

    $fileList = [];

    $iterator = new RecursiveDirectoryIterator($directory,
FilesystemIterator::SKIP_DOTS);

    foreach($iterator as $entry) {

        $fileName = $entry->getFilename();
```

```
            $dirFlag = $entry->isDir();

            if (!$dirFlag && $fileName[0] != '.') {
                $fileList[$fileName] = 'size is ' . $entry->getSize();
            } else {
                if ($dirFlag && $fileName[0] != '.') {
                    $fileList[$fileName] = getDirList(
                        $directory . DIRECTORY_SEPARATOR . $fileName,
                        $du
                    );
                }
            }

        }

    return $fileList;
}

$du = '';

$baseDirectory = dirname(__FILE__);

$fileList = getDirList($baseDirectory, $du);

echo '<html><head></head><body><p>';

echo 'Disk Usage : ' . $du . '<br /><br /><br />';

echo 'Directory Name : ' . $baseDirectory . '<br /><br />';

echo 'File listing :';

echo '</p><pre>';

print_r($fileList);

echo '</pre></body></html>';
```

Let's try profiling the new script (`chap2post.php`) in order to measure our improvements. Again, please browse to the following URL with Chrome to see the script's output and launch a profile using the Blackfire Companion:
`http://localhost:8181/chap2post.php`.

The results should be as follows:

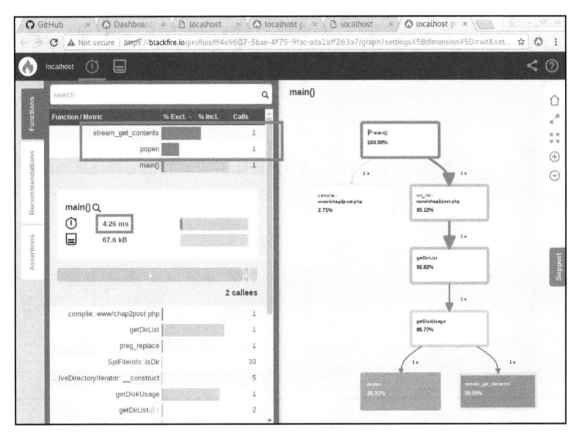

Now, the script takes only 4.26 ms to complete its execution and only one process was created using the 'popen' function

The result shows us that this script now has a wall time of **4.26 ms** and that the function `popen` is only creating one sub-process. Also, if we scroll down, we now notice that `SplInfo::getFilename` is only called thirty-three times which is two times less than before:

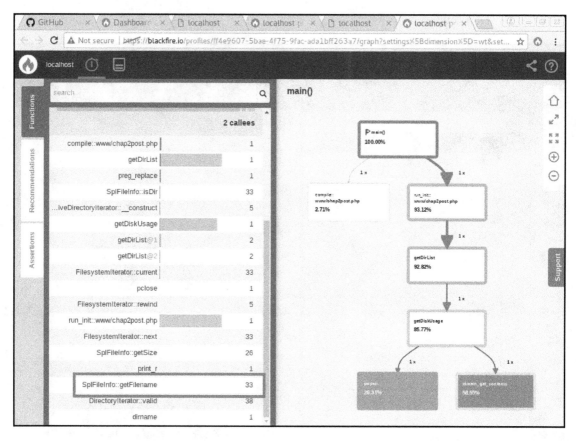

Now, the SplFileInfo::getFilename function gets called only 33 times

These are significant improvements, especially if this script is to be called thousands of times per minute on different directory structures. A good way to make sure that these improvements are not lost in future iterations of our application's development cycle would be to automate the profiler through performance tests. We will now give a quick example of how to automate performance testing with `Blackfire.io`.

Performance testing with Blackfire.io

Before we start, please note that this feature is available only to premium and enterprise users and that, therefore, it requires a paid subscription.

In order to automate performance testing, we will start by creating a very simple `blackfire.yml` file in our repository. This file will contain our tests. A test should be composed of a name, a regular expression and a set of assertions. It is always preferable to avoid creating volatile time tests as these make for very brittle tests that might yield very different results from one profiling session to the next. Examples of strong performance tests would be to check CPU or memory consumption, number of SQL queries or testing results by profile comparisons. In our case, we will create a very basic and volatile time test just for the sake of giving a short and simple example. Here is the content of our `.blackfire.yml` file:

```
tests:
    "Pages should be fast enough":
        path: "/.*" # run the assertions for all HTTP requests
        assertions:
            - "main.wall_time < 10ms" # wall clock time is less than 10ms
```

The final step would be to integrate this performance test with a continuous integration tool. To select the tool of your choice, please consult the documentation at the following URL: `https://blackfire.io/docs/integrations/index`.

In our case, we will integrate with *Travis CI*. To do so, we must create two files. One will include our credentials and must be encrypted (`.blackfire.travis.ini.enc`). The other will include our Travis instructions (`.travis.yml`).

Here is the content of our `.blackfire.travis.ini` file before encryption (replace the credentials with your own):

```
[blackfire]

server-id=BLACKFIRE_SERVER_ID
server-token=BLACKFIRE_SERVER_TOKEN
client-id=BLACKFIRE_CLIENT_ID
client-token=BLACKFIRE_CLIENT_TOKEN
endpoint=https://blackfire.io/
collector=https://blackfire.io/
```

This file must then be encrypted before being committed to your repository. To do so, please issue the following commands inside the Linux for PHP container:

```
# gem install travis
# travis encrypt-file /srv/www/.blackfire.travis.ini -r
[your_Github_repository_name_here]
```

Here is the content of our `.travis.yml` file:

```
language: php

matrix:
    include:
        - php: 5.6
        - php: 7.0
          env: BLACKFIRE=on

sudo: false

cache:
    - $HOME/.composer/cache/files

before_install:
    - if [[ "$BLACKFIRE" = "on" ]]; then
        openssl aes-256-cbc -K [ENCRYPT_KEY_HERE] -iv [ENCRYPT_IV_HERE] -in
.blackfire.travis.ini.enc -out ~/.blackfire.ini -d
        curl -L https://blackfire.io/api/v1/releases/agent/linux/amd64 |
tar zxpf -
        chmod 755 agent && ./agent --config=~/.blackfire.ini --
socket=unix:///tmp/blackfire.sock &
      fi

install:
    - travis_retry composer install

before_script:
    - phpenv config-rm xdebug.ini || true
    - if [[ "$BLACKFIRE" = "on" ]]; then
        curl -L
https://blackfire.io/api/v1/releases/probe/php/linux/amd64/$(php -r "echo
PHP_MAJOR_VERSION . PHP_MINOR_VERSION;")-zts | tar zxpf -
        echo "extension=$(pwd)/$(ls blackfire-*.so | tr -d '[[:space:]]')"
> ~/.phpenv/versions/$(phpenv version-name)/etc/conf.d/blackfire.ini
        echo "blackfire.agent_socket=unix:///tmp/blackfire.sock" >>
~/.phpenv/versions/$(phpenv version-name)/etc/conf.d/blackfire.ini
      fi
```

```
script:
    - phpunit
```

Once committed, this configuration will ensure that the performance tests will run on each git push to your Github repository. Thus, performance becomes a feature and is continuously tested like any other of your application's features. The next step is to monitor your code's performance after deployment on a production server. Let's discover some of the available tools in order to do so.

Monitoring performance with the TICK Stack

The TICK Stack was developed by InfluxData (*InfluxDB*) and is made of a series of integrated components that allow you to easily process time-series data generated by different services through time. TICK is an acronym that is composed of the first letters of each main product of the monitoring suite. T is for Telegraf, which collects the information we wish to obtain on our production server. I is for InfluxDB, which is a time-series database that contains the information collected by Telegraf or by any other application which is configured to do so. C is for Chronograf, a graph tool that allows us to easily understand the collected data. Finally, K is for Kapacitor, an alert automation tool.

Monitoring infrastructure performance is not only important to determine if applications and scripts are running as expected, but also allows for development of more advanced algorithms such as failure prediction and unexpected behavior pattern recognition, thus making it possible to automate many aspects of performance monitoring.

Of course, there are many other great performance monitoring tools, like Prometheus and Graphite, but we decided to use the TICK stack instead, because we are more interested in doing event logging than doing pure metrics. For more information on what the TICK stack is, how it works internally and what it is used for, please read this very informative article by Gianluca Arbezzano published on the Codeship website: `https://blog.codeship.com/infrastructure-monitoring-with-tick-stack/`.

Now, in order to see how useful our `Blackfire.io` supported analysis was and how much more efficient our code has become, we will run the two scripts again but, this time, while using copies of the official TICK Docker images so that we may monitor any improvement in the Web server's overall performance once the optimized PHP script is deployed on it. We will also be replacing Chronograf with Grafana, a highly customizable graph tool, and we will not be setting up Kapacitor, since configuring alerts is slightly beyond the scope of our current objectives.

Let's begin by activating `mod_status` on our Apache server. From our Linux for PHP's CLI, enter the following commands:

```
# sed -i 's/#Include \/etc\/httpd\/extra\/httpd-info.conf/Include
\/etc\/httpd\/extra\/httpd-info.conf/' /etc/httpd/httpd.conf
# sed -i 's/Require ip 127/Require ip 172/' /etc/httpd/extra/httpd-
info.conf
# /etc/init.d/httpd restart
```

Once you have done this, you should be able to see the server's status report by browsing with Chrome to the following URL: `http://localhost:8181/server-status?auto`.

The next step is to launch the TICK suite. Please open two new Terminal windows in order to do so.

In the first Terminal window, type this command:

```
# docker run -d --name influxdb -p 8086:8086 andrewscaya/influxdb
```

Then, in the second newly opened Terminal window, get the IP addresses of our two containers by issuing this command:

```
# docker network inspect bridge
```

Here is the result of this command on my computer:

The IP addresses of the two containers

Please retain these two addresses as they will be needed to configure Telegraf and Grafana.

We will now generate a sample configuration file for Telegraf with a simple command (this step is optional, as a sample file is already included in this book's repository).

Firstly, change the directory to our project's working directory (Git repository) and enter the following command:

```
# docker run --rm andrewscaya/telegraf –sample-config > telegraf.conf
```

Secondly, open the new file with your favorite editor and uncomment the following lines in the inputs.apache section. Do not forget to enter our Linux *for PHP* container's IP address on the urls line:

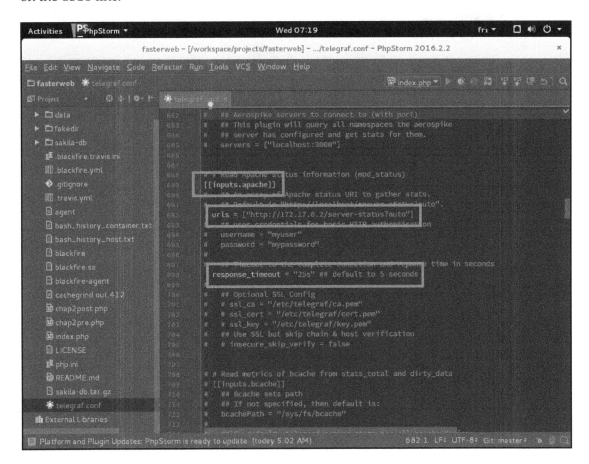

Configuring Telegraf in order to have it monitor the Apache server running in the other container

In the Terminal window, we can now launch Telegraf with this command (please make sure that you are in our project's working directory):

```
# docker run --net=container:influxdb -v
${PWD}/telegraf.conf:/etc/telegraf/telegraf.conf:ro andrewscaya/telegraf
```

In the second newly spawned Terminal window, launch Grafana with the following command:

```
# docker run -d --name grafana -p 3000:3000 andrewscaya/grafana
```

With Chrome, browse to `http://localhost:3000/login`. You will see Grafana's login page. Please authenticate with the **User** admin using the **Password** admin:

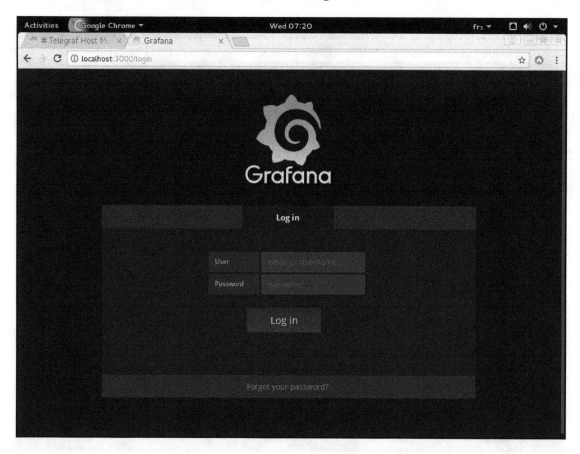

The Grafana login page is displayed

Then, add a new data source:

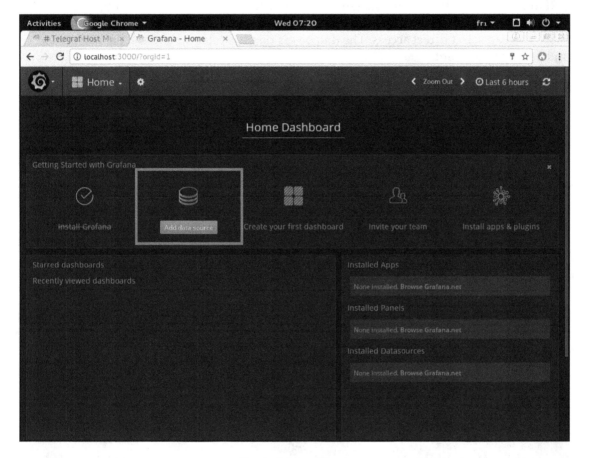

Connecting Grafana to a data source

Please choose a name for the InfluxDB data source. Select **InfluxDB** as the type. Enter the URL for the InfluxDB container instance, which includes the IP address that you obtained in one of our previous steps, followed by the default port number for InfluxDB, which is 8086. You can select **direct** access. The database's name is **telegraf** and the database's user and password are **root**:

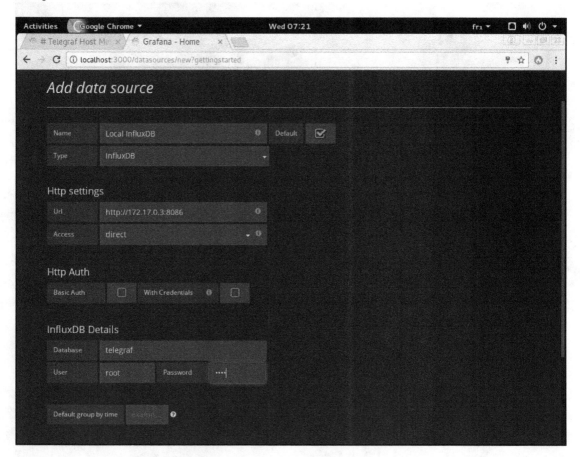

Configuring Grafana's data source

Finally, click the **Add** button:

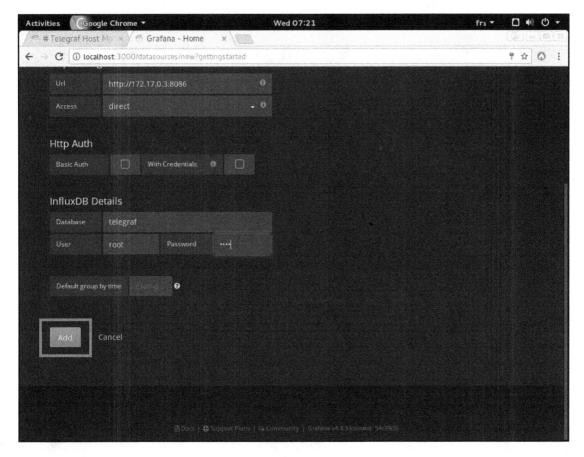

Adding the data source

Now that the data source has been added, let's add a couple of dashboards that we will import from the Grafana website. Start by clicking **Import** under the **Dashboards** menu entry:

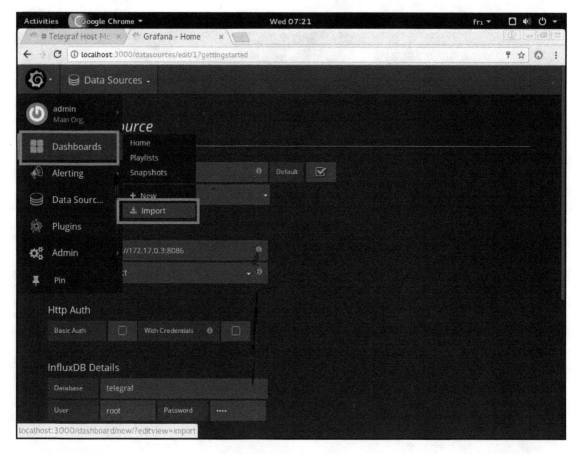

Click on the import menu item to begin importing dashboards

The two dashboards that we will add are the following:

- Telegraf Host Metrics (`https://grafana.com/dashboards/1443`):

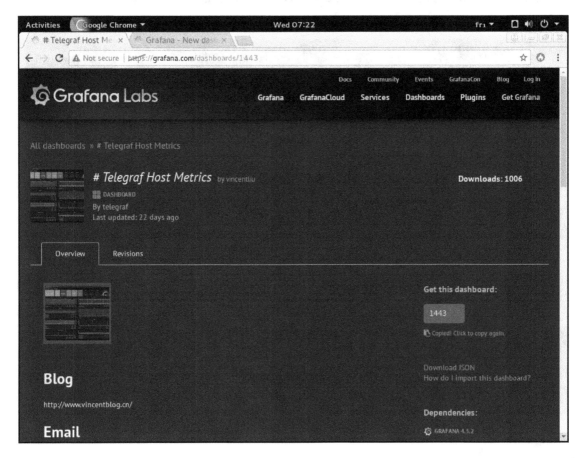

The homepage of the Telegraf Host Metrics dashboard

- Apache Overview (`https://grafana.com/dashboards/331`):

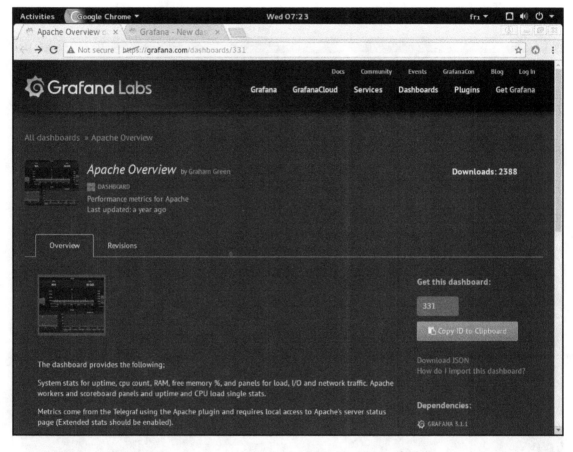

The homepage of the Apache Overview dashboard

On the import screen, simply enter the number of the dashboard and click **Load**:

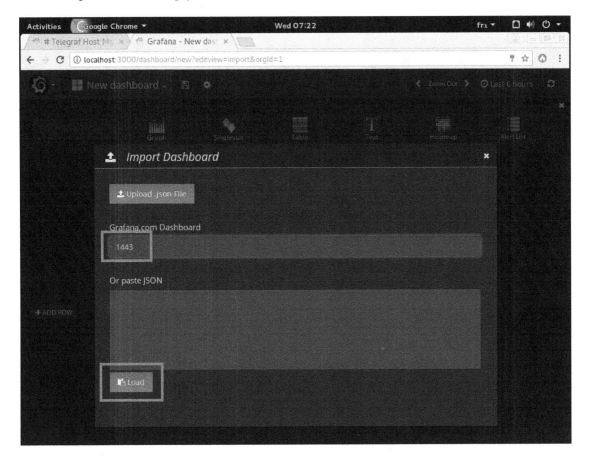

Loading the Telegraf Host Metrics dashboard

Then, confirm the name of the new dashboard and select our **Local InfluxDB** connection:

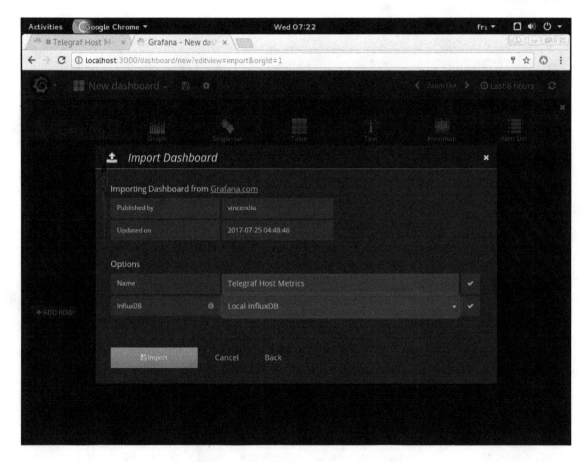

Connecting the Telegraf Host Metrics dashboard to the InfluxDB data source

You should now see the new dashboard:

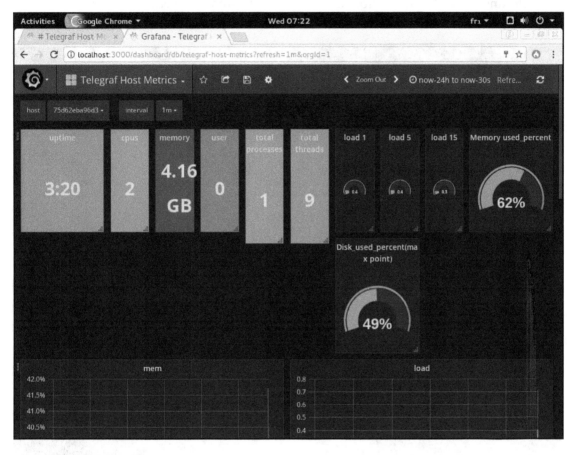

The Telegraf Host Metrics dashboard is displayed

We will now repeat the final two steps in order to import the Apache Overview dashboard. After clicking on the **Import** button under the **Dashboards** menu entry, enter the dashboard's identifier (331) and click the **Load** button:

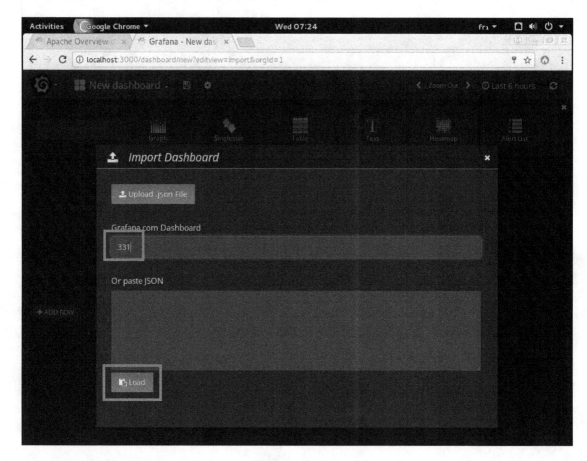

Loading the Apache Overview dashboard

Then, confirm the name and select our **Local InfluxDB** data source:

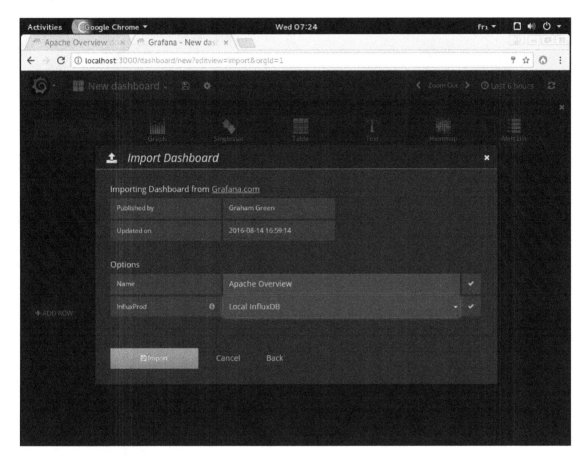

Connecting the Apache Overview dashboard to the InfluxDB data source

You should now see the second dashboard in the browser:

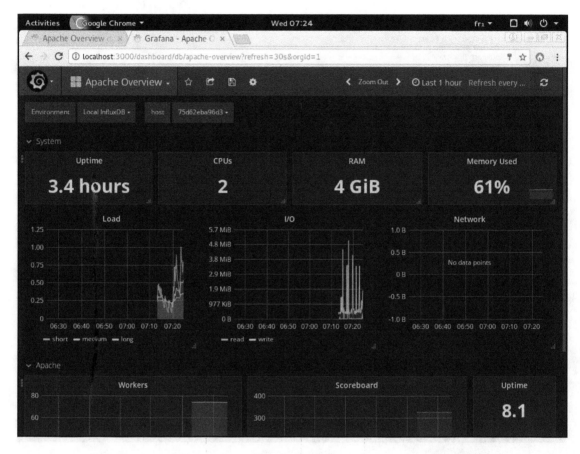

The Apache Overview dashboard is displayed

All TICK suite dashboards allow for more advanced configuration and customization of graphs. It would therefore be possible to collect a custom set of time-series data points through the execution of custom cron scripts for example, and then configure the dashboards to display this data as you see fit.

In the case of our current example, the TICK suite is now installed and configured. Thus, we can begin testing and monitoring the PHP script that was optimized using `Blackfire.io` in the first part of this chapter in order to measure the changes in its performance. We will start by deploying, benchmarking and monitoring the old version. On the Linux for PHP's CLI, enter the following command in order to benchmark the old version of the script:

```
# siege -b -c 3000 -r 100 localhost/chap2pre.php
```

The benchmark test should yield something similar to the following result:

```
                    vagrant@zend: /workspace/projects/fasterweb                    x

 File  Edit  View  Search  Terminal  Help
HTTP/1.1 200      0.05 secs:     2000 bytes ==> GET   /chap2pre.php
HTTP/1.1 200      0.05 secs:     2000 bytes ==> GET   /chap2pre.php
HTTP/1.1 200      0.06 secs:     2000 bytes ==> GET   /chap2pre.php
HTTP/1.1 200      0.06 secs:     2000 bytes ==> GET   /chap2pre.php
HTTP/1.1 200      0.04 secs:     2000 bytes ==> GET   /chap2pre.php
HTTP/1.1 200      0.04 secs:     2000 bytes ==> GET   /chap2pre.php
HTTP/1.1 200      0.03 secs:     2000 bytes ==> GET   /chap2pre.php
HTTP/1.1 200      0.02 secs:     2000 bytes ==> GET   /chap2pre.php
HTTP/1.1 200      0.02 secs:     2000 bytes ==> GET   /chap2pre.php

Transactions:                  25189  hits
Availability:                  98.78 %
Elapsed time:                 350.83 secs
Data transferred:              48.13 MB
Response time:                  2.97 secs
Transaction rate:              71.80 trans/sec
Throughput:                     0.14 MB/sec
Concurrency:                   213.22
Successful transactions:       25189
Failed transactions:             311
Longest transaction:           76.47
Shortest transaction:           0.02

root@791f838c1bab [ / ]#
```

The results of the performance benchmark of the original script are displayed

Then, after waiting approximately ten minutes, start benchmarking the new version of the script by entering the following command:

```
# siege -b -c 3000 -r 100 localhost/chap2post.php
```

Here is the result of this latest benchmark on my computer:

```
vagrant@zend: /workspace/projects/fasterweb                          ×

 File   Edit   View   Search   Terminal   Help
HTTP/1.1 200      0.00 secs:     2000 bytes ==> GET   /chap2post.php
HTTP/1.1 200      0.01 secs:     2000 bytes ==> GET   /chap2post.php
HTTP/1.1 200      0.00 secs:     2000 bytes ==> GET   /chap2post.php
HTTP/1.1 200      0.00 secs:     2000 bytes ==> GET   /chap2post.php
HTTP/1.1 200      0.01 secs:     2000 bytes ==> GET   /chap2post.php
HTTP/1.1 200      0.00 secs:     2000 bytes ==> GET   /chap2post.php
HTTP/1.1 200      0.00 secs:     2000 bytes ==> GET   /chap2post.php
HTTP/1.1 200      0.01 secs:     2000 bytes ==> GET   /chap2post.php
HTTP/1.1 200      0.01 secs:     2000 bytes ==> GET   /chap2post.php

Transactions:              25432 hits
Availability:              99.73 %
Elapsed time:              101.33 secs
Data transferred:          48.53 MB
Response time:             0.82 secs
Transaction rate:          250.98 trans/sec
Throughput:                0.48 MB/sec
Concurrency:               204.66
Successful transactions:   25432
Failed transactions:          68
Longest transaction:       67.21
Shortest transaction:      0.01

root@791f838c1bab [ / ]#
```

The results of the performance benchmark of the optimized script are displayed

The results already reveal to us a considerable improvement in performance. Indeed, the new script allows for more than three times the number of transactions per second and more than three times fewer failed transactions.

Now, let's have a look at what data our TICK Stack collected concerning the performance of these two versions of our PHP script:

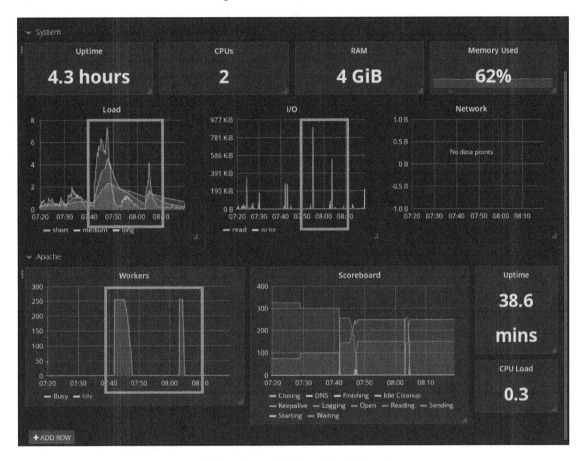

The gain in performance is clearly seen in the monitoring graphs

The graphs in our Grafana dashboard clearly show a performance boost of the same order of magnitude as the benchmark results themselves. The benchmark test launched after **08:00** against the new version of our script clearly generated two times less load on the server, caused two times less input (I/O) and was more than three times faster in general than the old version that was benchmarked previously around **7:40**. Therefore, our `Blackfire.io` optimizations have, without a doubt, made the new version of our PHP script more efficient.

Summary

In this chapter, we have learned how to install and configure a basic `Blackfire.io` setup in order to easily and automatically profile code when committing it to a repository. We have also explored how to install a TICK Stack in order to continuously monitor our code's performance after its deployment on a live production server. Thus, we have seen how to install and configure profiling and monitoring tools that help us easily optimize PHP code in a **continuous integration** (**CI**) and a **continuous deployment** (**CD**) environment.

In the next chapter, we will explore how better understanding PHP data structures and using simplified functions can help an application's global performance along its critical execution path. We will start by analyzing a project's critical path and, then, fine-tune certain of its data structures and functions.

References

[1] For further explanations on these performance testing terms, please go to this URL: `https://blackfire.io/docs/reference-guide/time`.

Harnessing the Power of PHP 7 Data Structures and Functions

In this chapter, we will learn how to harness PHP 7's performance boosts using most of its key optimizations.

Also, we will explore how better understanding data structures and datatypes, and how using simplified functions can help a PHP application's global performance along its critical execution path.

Moreover, we will learn how it is best to avoid using inefficient structures, like most dynamic ones, in our PHP code.

Finally, although PHP is not a functional language, we will see how some functional techniques can be of immediate help when optimizing PHP code.

Thus, in this chapter, we will cover the following points:

- PHP 7 optimizations
- Identifying possible optimizations and avoiding dynamic structures
- Functional programming and memoization

PHP 7 optimizations

PHP 7 is in itself a major optimization. A good part of PHP's code base was rewritten for this release and most official benchmarks show that, generally speaking, almost any PHP code will run about two times faster or more with PHP 7 than with previous versions.

PHP is programmed in C and optimizing the performance of Zend's **Ahead-Of-Time** (**AOT**) compiler depends ultimately on using the C compiler's internal logic in an optimized way. This latest version of PHP is the result of many years of research and experiments by Zend. The greater part of these optimizations was implemented by eliminating the performance overhead generated by certain PHP internal structural constructs and data structures. According to *Dmitry Stogov[1], a typical real-life PHP application spends about 20% of the CPU time in the memory manager, 10% doing hash table operations, 30% in internal functions and only 30% in the VM*. In order to optimize the execution of PHP code, PHP 7's new version of the Zend Engine had to start by representing source code in an **Abstract Syntax Tree** (**AST**), thus allowing the engine to generate better quality **Intermediate Representations** (**IR**) of the source code and, since PHP 7.1, to be able to remove dead code and reduce as many expressions as possible to their static representation through **Static Single Assignment** (**SSA**) form and type inference. In turn, this allows the engine to only allocate necessary data structures to the stack instead of the heap in memory at runtime.

This is very important in order to understand the rest of this chapter, as it allows us to see why datatype juggling and dynamic structures in general will create most of the overhead by bloating memory allocation at runtime, why certain data structures had to be re-implemented to allow for C-level performance and why immutability is a developer's ally when trying to achieve better code performance. Let's have a look at these elements more closely.

Strict typing

When a language is dynamically typed, that is to say, it has loosely typed variables, it provides a higher level of abstraction that boosts the developer's productivity, but doesn't offer the best performance since its compiler has more work to do when trying to determine the datatypes of its variables. It comes as no surprise that strongly typed languages have always had better performance at runtime than loosely typed ones. This conclusion was confirmed by Facebook's HipHop project, which conducted benchmark tests with different languages and came to the conclusion that statically compiled languages always execute more quickly and consume less memory than dynamic ones.

Although PHP 7 is still a loosely typed language, it now offers the possibility to strict type variables and function signatures. This can be easily tested by executing the following code example. Let's run the following code to see its current performance:

```php
// chap3_strict_typing.php

declare(strict_types = 0);

$start = microtime(true);

function test ($variable)
{
    $variable++;

    return "$variable is a test.";
}

ob_start();

for ($x = 0; $x < 1000000; $x++) {

    $array[$x] = (string) $x;

    echo test($array[$x]) . PHP_EOL;

}

$time = microtime(true) - $start;

ob_clean();

ob_end_flush();

echo 'Time elapsed: ' . $time . PHP_EOL;
```

Here are the results of running this script using `Blackfire.io`:

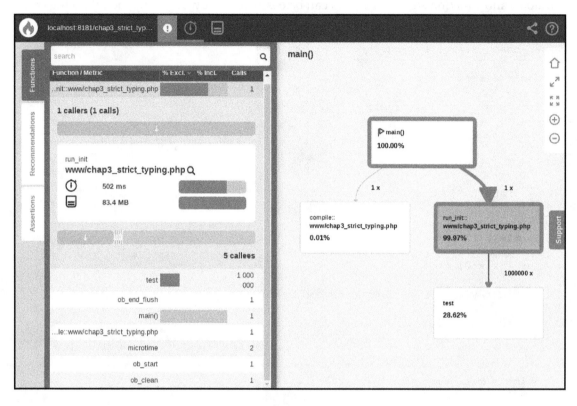

The profiling report when omitting to do strict typing of variables and function signatures

Now, let's replace the code with the following:

```
// chap3_strict_typing_modified.php

declare(strict_types = 1);

$start = microtime(true);

function test (int $variable) : string
{
    $variable++;

    return $variable . ' is a test.';
}

ob_start();
```

```
for ($x = 0; $x < 1000000; $x++) {

    $array[$x] = (int) $x;

    echo test($array[$x]) . PHP_EOL;

}

$time = microtime(true) - $start;

ob_clean();

ob_end_flush();

echo 'Time elapsed: ' . $time . PHP_EOL;
```

If we execute it, we will immediately see the difference in performance:

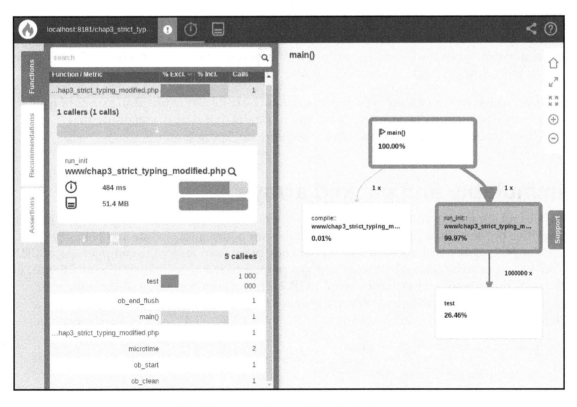

The profiling report when strict typing variables and function signatures

The performance boost can also be seen using the `microtime()` function. Let's run both versions of our script and see the result:

```
                    vagrant@zend: /workspace/projects/fasterweb                    ×

 File  Edit  View  Search  Terminal  Help
root@8f23640bf88f [ /srv/www ]# php chap3_strict_typing.php
Time elapsed: 0.20446491241455
root@8f23640bf88f [ /srv/www ]# php chap3_strict_typing_modified.php
Time elapsed: 0.16548204421997
root@8f23640bf88f [ /srv/www ]# █
```

Comparing script performance with the microtime() function

In order to fully benefit from PHP's new AST and SSA features, developers should try to strictly type variables and function signatures as much as possible. This will become especially true when the Zend Engine gets, in future releases, a **Just-In-Time** (**JIT**) compiler as this will allow for further optimizations solely based on type inference.

Also, an added bonus of strict typing is that it lets the compiler manage an aspect of code quality by eliminating the necessity of having unit tests that simply make sure that functions are behaving as expected when receiving unexpected inputs.

Immutable and packed arrays

As we will see later in this chapter, immutability not only helps the developer lessen his cognitive burden while programming and makes for better quality code and better unit tests in general, but will also allow for better code optimizations by the compiler. As of PHP 7, any static array is cached by OPcache and a pointer to the array is shared with any part of the code that tries to access it. Moreover, PHP 7 offers a very important optimization for packed arrays, which are arrays that are indexed with ascending integers only. Let's take the following code and execute it against PHP 5.6 and then PHP 7 with OPcache enabled:

```php
// chap3_immutable_arrays.php

$start = microtime(true);

for ($x = 0; $x < 10000; $x++) {
    $array[] = [
        'key1' => 'This is the first key',
```

```
        'key2' => 'This is the second key',
        'key3' => 'This is the third key',
    ];
}

echo $array[8181]['key2'] . PHP_EOL;

$time = microtime(true) - $start;

echo 'Time elapsed: ' . $time . PHP_EOL;

echo memory_get_usage() . ' bytes' . PHP_EOL;
```

If we run the previous code with PHP 5.6, we consume almost 7.4 MB of memory and the elapsed time is 0.005 seconds:

The results when running the script against PHP 5.6

If we run the same code with PHP 7, we get the following result:

The results when running the same script against PHP 7.1

The results are impressive. The same script is 40 times faster and consumes almost 10 times less memory. Immutable arrays therefore provide more speed and developers should avoid modifying large arrays and encourage the use of packed arrays as much as possible when dealing with large arrays in order to optimize memory allocation and maximize speed at runtime.

Memory allocation of integers and floats

Another optimization introduced by PHP 7 is the reuse of previously allocated variable containers. If you need to create a large number of variables, you should try to reuse them, as PHP 7's compiler will avoid reallocating memory and reuse the memory slots that are already allocated. Let's have a look at the following example:

```
// chap3_variables.php

$start = microtime(true);

for ($x = 0; $x < 10000; $x++) {
    $$x = 'test';
}

for ($x = 0; $x < 10000; $x++) {
    $$x = $x;
}

$time = microtime(true) - $start;

echo 'Time elapsed: ' . $time . PHP_EOL;

echo memory_get_usage() . ' bytes' . PHP_EOL;
```

Let's run this code against PHP 5.6 and PHP 7 in order to see the difference in memory consumption. Let's start with PHP 5.6:

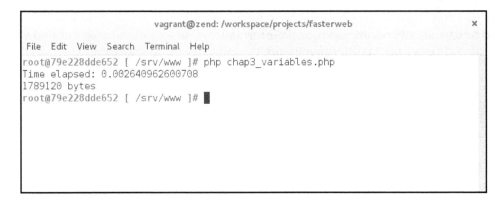

The results when running the script against PHP 5.6

Now, let's run the same script with PHP 7:

The results when running the same script against PHP 7.1

As you can see, the results show us that memory consumption was reduced by almost a third. Although this goes against the very principle of the immutability of variables, it is still a very important optimization when you must allocate a large number of variables in memory.

String interpolation and concatenation

In PHP 7, string interpolation has been optimized with a new string analysis algorithm. This means that string interpolation is now much faster than concatenation and that what used to be true about concatenation and performance is no longer the case. Let's take the following code example in order to measure the new algorithm's performance:

```php
// chap3_string_interpolation.php

$a = str_repeat(chr(rand(48, 122)), rand(1024, 3000));

$b = str_repeat(chr(rand(48, 122)), rand(1024, 3000));

$start = microtime(true);

for ($x = 0; $x < 10000; $x++) {
    $$x = "$a is not $b";
}

$time = microtime(true) - $start;

echo 'Time elapsed: ' . $time . PHP_EOL;

echo memory_get_usage() . ' bytes' . PHP_EOL;
```

Here are the performance measurements when running this code against PHP 5.6:

vagrant@zend: /workspace/projects/fasterweb

File   Edit   View   Search   Terminal   Help

```
root@79e228dde652 [ /srv/www ]# php chap3_string_interpolation.php
Time elapsed: 0.021815061569214
52117120 bytes
root@79e228dde652 [ /srv/www ]#
```

The results when running the script against PHP 5.6

And here is the same script with PHP 7:

The results when running the same script against PHP 7.1

PHP 7 is about three to four times faster and consumes more than a third less memory. The lesson to be learned here is to try using PHP 7's string interpolation algorithm as much as possible when dealing with strings.

Parameter references

Even though it is best to avoid passing a variable by reference to a function in order to avoid altering your application's state outside of the function, PHP 7 makes it possible to pass variables by reference to functions in a highly optimized way even if the reference is a mismatch. Let's take the following code example in order to better understand how PHP 7 is much more efficient in doing so than PHP 5:

```php
// chap3_references.php

$start = microtime(true);

function test (&$byRefVar)
{
    $test = $byRefVar;
}

$variable = array_fill(0, 10000, 'banana');

for ($x = 0; $x < 10000; $x++) {
    test($variable);
}
```

```
$time = microtime(true) - $start;

echo 'Time elapsed: ' . $time . PHP_EOL;

echo memory_get_usage() . ' bytes' . PHP_EOL;
```

Let's run this code with the PHP 5 binary:

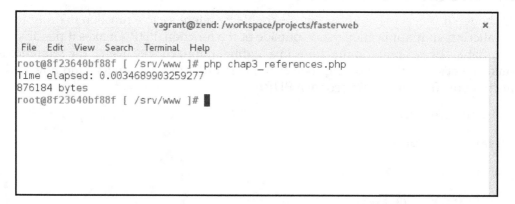

The results when running the script against PHP 5.6

Here is the result when executing the same code with PHP 7:

The results when running the same script against PHP 7.1

The results are once more very impressive as PHP 7 does the same work with almost a third less memory allocation and 1,000 times faster! What is happening under the hood is that PHP 7 no longer makes copies in memory of variables when a reference mismatch occurs. Thus, the new compiler avoids bloating memory allocation for nothing and speeds up the execution of any PHP script where reference mismatches are an issue.

Identifying more possible optimizations

When optimizing an application, you will start by identifying the most time-consuming functions, especially along the application's critical path. As stated in a previous chapter, most of those functions will be I/O functions as these are always the most expensive operations for a computer to execute. Most of the time you will see the possibility to optimize loops and reduce the number of system calls, but you will soon realize that I/O operations remain costly no matter what optimizations you wish to bring to them. Sometimes, though, you might run into very slow PHP structures that can simply be replaced with faster ones, or you may realize that poorly designed code can easily be refactored to be less resource-hungry, such as when replacing a dynamic structure with a simpler static one.

Indeed, dynamic structures should be avoided unless absolutely necessary. We will now have a look at a very simple example. We will program the same functionality four times, but with three different approaches: functional and dynamic, functional and static, and finally, structural and static. Let's start with the functional and dynamic approach:

```php
// chap3_dynamic_1.php

$start = microtime(true);

$x = 1;

$data = [];

$populateArray = function ($populateArray, $data, $x) {

    $data[$x] = $x;

    $x++;

    return $x <= 1000 ? $populateArray($populateArray, $data, $x) : $data;

};

$data = $populateArray($populateArray, $data, $x);

$time = microtime(true) - $start;

echo 'Time elapsed: ' . $time . PHP_EOL;

echo memory_get_usage() . ' bytes' . PHP_EOL;
```

This code creates an array with 1,000 elements by calling the same closure recursively. If we run this code, we get the following result:

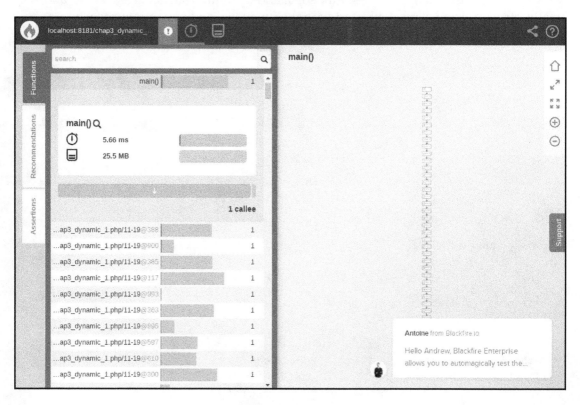

Time elapsed and memory consumed when running the script programmed with the functional and dynamic approach

Let's have a look at the results of running this script using `Blackfire.io`:

The profiling report when running the script programmed with the functional and dynamic approach

Let's code the same functionality, but in a more static fashion with a classic named function instead:

```
// chap3_dynamic_2.php

$start = microtime(true);

$x = 1;

$data = [];

function populateArray(Array $data, $x)
{
    $data[$x] = $x;

    $x++;

    return $x <= 1000 ? populateArray($data, $x) : $data;
}

$data = populateArray($data, $x);

$time = microtime(true) - $start;

echo 'Time elapsed: ' . $time . PHP_EOL;

echo memory_get_usage() . ' bytes' . PHP_EOL;
```

If we execute this version of our code, we obtain the following result:

Time elapsed and memory consumed when running the script programmed with the functional and static approach

Running the script with the `Blackfire.io` profiler yields these results:

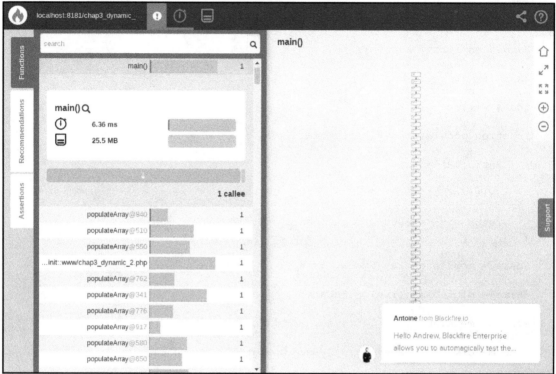

The profiling report when running the script programmed with the functional and static approach

Finally, let's program this functionality again, but in a very structural and static way by using a `for` loop instead of tail-calling the function recursively:

```
// chap3_dynamic_3.php

$start = microtime(true);

$data = [];

function populateArray(Array $data)
{
    static $x = 1;

    $data[$x] = $x;

    $x++;
```

```
        return $data;
}

for ($x = 1; $x <= 1000; $x++) {
        $data = populateArray($data);
}

$time = microtime(true) - $start;

echo 'Time elapsed: ' . $time . PHP_EOL;

echo memory_get_usage() . ' bytes' . PHP_EOL;
```

Here are the results after executing this latest version of the code:

Time elapsed and memory consumed when running the script programmed with the structural and static approach

Here are the results of profiling this version of the script with `Blackfire.io`:

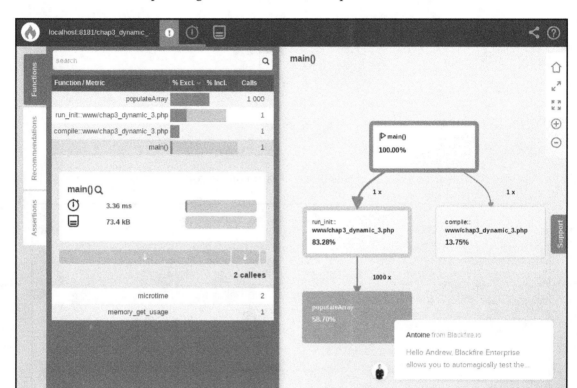

The profiling report when running the script programmed with the structural and static approach

The results clearly show that the structural approach is the fastest. If we now go a little further down the structural route, with only a hint of functional programming, and try using a generator to create the array iteratively, we should not be surprised by the high performance results that we will get. Here is the last version of our code:

```php
// chap3_dynamic_4.php

$start = microtime(true);

$data = [];

function populateArray()
{
    for ($i = 1; $i <= 1000; $i++) {

        yield $i => $i;
```

```
    }

    return;
}

foreach (populateArray() as $key => $value) {

    $data[$key] = $value;

}

$time = microtime(true) - $start;

echo 'Time elapsed: ' . $time . PHP_EOL;

echo memory_get_usage() . ' bytes' . PHP_EOL;
```

This is the result when running the latest version of our code:

```
                    vagrant@zend: /workspace/projects/fasterweb              ×

 File  Edit  View  Search  Terminal  Help
root@6c9d0310ab84 [ /srv/www ]# php chap3_dynamic_4.php
Time elapsed: 6.103515625E-5
385064 bytes
root@6c9d0310ab84 [ /srv/www ]# █



```

Time elapsed and memory consumed when running the script programmed with a very structural and static approach

Here are the results with `Blackfire.io`:

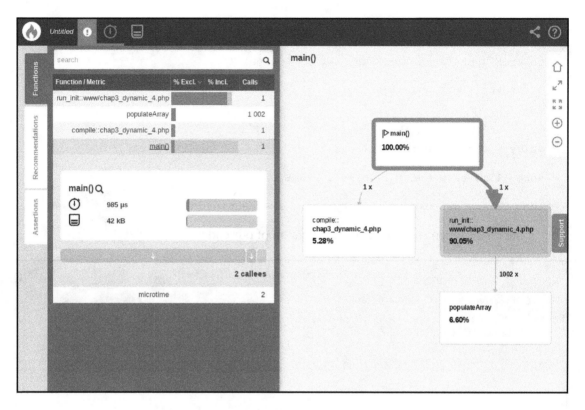

The profiling report when running the script programmed with a very structural and static approach

The results clearly show how this last version of our code really outperforms the other ones. Indeed, PHP is still a very structural language as its compiler still does not fully optimize tail-recursion calls and does take less time to complete the execution of a program if it is coded in a structural way. Does this mean that PHP will never be a functional language and that it is best to avoid programming in a functional way in PHP? The short answer is no. Also, does this mean that functional programming with PHP is a thing of the future only? Again, the answer is no. There are certain functional programming techniques that we can use immediately and that will help our scripts be more performant. Let's have a look at one in particular, which is memoization.

Functional programming and memoization

PHP is an imperative and not a declarative language, which means that programming is done using statements that alter the state of the program, just like other languages in the C family, and it is not composed of stateless expressions or declarations, like SQL for example. Though PHP is primarily a structural (procedural) and object-oriented programming language, we have seen, since PHP 5.3, more and more requests for change that asked for more and more structures that are functional in nature, such as generators and lambda functions (anonymous functions). Nevertheless, PHP remains for now a structural language in nature, especially when it comes to performance.

This being said, most functional programming techniques will yield fruit a few years from now, but there are still some functional programming techniques that can be used immediately in PHP that will improve performance as soon as you implement them in the code base of a project. One such technique is memoization.

Memoization is a functional programming technique in which the result of an expensive functional computation is stored and reused each time it is called within the same program. The idea is to return the static value of a function when it receives a certain input. Obviously, to avoid the invalidation of values, the function should be referentially transparent, which means that it should always return the same output when given a specific input. Of course, this comes in handy when you realize that a referentially transparent function is called many times along the critical path of an application and is computed every time. Memoization is an easy optimization to implement as it simply creates a cache to store the results of the computation.

Let's look at a simple example that will help us easily grasp the idea behind it. Let's say we have the following code along the critical path of an application:

```php
// chap3_memoization_before.php

$start = microtime(true);

$x = 1;

$data = [];

function populateArray(Array $data, $x)
{
    $data[$x] = $x;

    $x++;

    return $x <= 1000 ? populateArray($data, $x) : $data;
```

```
}

$data = populateArray($data, $x);

$data = populateArray($data, $x);

$data = populateArray($data, $x);

$data = populateArray($data, $x);

$data = populateArray($data, $x);

$time = microtime(true) - $start;

echo 'Time elapsed: ' . $time . PHP_EOL;

echo memory_get_usage() . ' bytes' . PHP_EOL;
```

Here, we see that the same function is called recursively many times. Moreover, it is a referentially transparent function. Therefore, it is a perfect candidate for memoization.

Let's start by checking its performance. If we execute the code, we will get the following result:

The results before implementing memoization

Now, let's implement a cache to memoize the results:

```php
// chap3_memoization_after.php

$start = microtime(true);

$x = 1;

$data = [];

function populateArray(Array $data, $x)
{
    static $cache = [];

    static $key;

    if (!isset($key)) {
        $key = md5(serialize($x));
    }

    if (!isset($cache[$key])) {

        $data[$x] = $x;

        $x++;

        $cache[$key] = $x <= 1000 ? populateArray($data, $x) : $data;

    }

    return $cache[$key];

}

$data = populateArray($data, $x);

$data = populateArray($data, $x);

$data = populateArray($data, $x);

$data = populateArray($data, $x);

$data = populateArray($data, $x);

$time = microtime(true) - $start;
```

```
echo 'Time elapsed: ' . $time . PHP_EOL;

echo memory_get_usage() . ' bytes' . PHP_EOL;
```

Here are the results when executing this new version of the same code:

```
vagrant@zend: /workspace/projects/fasterweb                          ✕

 File  Edit  View  Search  Terminal  Help
root@97dab727455f [ /srv/www ]# php chap3_memoization_after.php
Time elapsed: 0.0059709548950195
387920 bytes
root@97dab727455f [ /srv/www ]#
```

The results after implementing memoization

As we can see, the PHP script now runs much faster. The more often a referentially transparent function is called along the critical path of your application, the more the speed will increase when using memoization. Let's have a look at our script's performance using `Blackfire.io`.

Here are the results when executing the script without memoization:

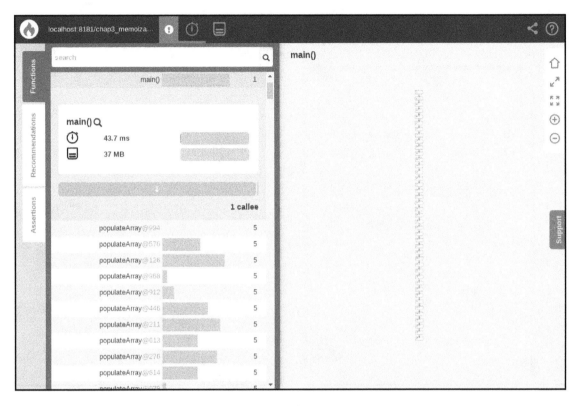

The profiling report when not using memoization

Here are the results with memoization:

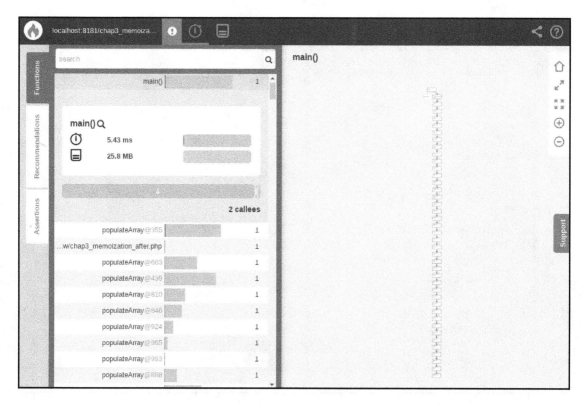

The profiling report when using memoization

The comparison shows that the memoized version of the script runs about eight times faster and consumes a third less memory. An important gain in performance for such an easy implementation.

One final question concerning memoization might be: can we cache the result between runs of the same script? Of course we can. It is up to you to determine the best way to cache it. You can use any standard way of caching a result. Also, there is at least one library that you can use to cache memoized results in PHP. You will find it at the following address: https://github.com/koktut/php-memoize. Please be aware that this library would not have been a good option for our last script as it doesn't work well with recursive tail-calls.

Summary

In this chapter, we have learned how PHP 7 is an optimization in itself, how avoiding dynamic structures in general will always boost the performance of your PHP scripts and how certain functional programming techniques such as memoization can be strong allies when optimizing code performance.

In the next chapter, we will learn how to cope with input and output (I/O) poor latency by learning about generators and asynchronous non-blocking code, multithreading with the POSIX threads (`pthreads`) library and multitasking with the `ReactPHP` library.

Reference

```
http://news.php.net/php.internals/73888
```

4
Envisioning the Future with Asynchronous PHP

In this chapter, we will learn how to determine what are the best strategies when coping with I/O calls and how to implement these strategies. We will see what distinguishes multithreading from multitasking, when to implement one or the other, and how to do it.

Also, we will learn how to use the `ReactPHP` library and how to benefit from event-driven programming when dealing with asynchronous I/O calls.

Thus, in this chapter, we will cover the following points:

- Optimizing I/O calls with asynchronous non-blocking code
- Multithreading with the `POSIX Threads` library
- Implementing a `ReactPHP` solution

Asynchronous non-blocking I/O calls

As we have seen in the previous chapters of this book, I/O calls will always offer the worst performance due to the underlying latency of establishing, using and closing streams and sockets. Since PHP is basically a synchronous language that waits for a called function to return before resuming code execution, I/O calls are especially problematic if the called function has to wait for a stream to close before returning to the calling code. This becomes even worse when a PHP application has thousands of I/O calls to do every few minutes for example.

Since PHP 5.3, it has become possible to interrupt PHP's normal flow of execution by using generators and thus, to execute code asynchronously. As we have seen previously, even if dynamic structures can be less performant in general, they can still be useful in speeding up blocking code. This is particularly true for I/O calls that usually have very high latency. In order to better grasp the orders of magnitude of I/O latency, we can consult the following well-known graph published by Google:

```
Latency Comparison Numbers
--------------------------
L1 cache reference 0.5 ns
Branch mispredict 5 ns
L2 cache reference 7 ns 14x L1 cache
Mutex lock/unlock 25 ns
Main memory reference 100 ns 20x L2 cache, 200x L1 cache
Compress 1K bytes with Zippy 3,000 ns 3 us
Send 1K bytes over 1 Gbps network 10,000 ns 10 us
Read 4K randomly from SSD* 150,000 ns 150 us ~1GB/sec SSD
Read 1 MB sequentially from memory 250,000 ns 250 us
Round trip within same data center 500,000 ns 500 us
Read 1 MB sequentially from SSD* 1,000,000 ns 1,000 us 1 ms ~1GB/sec SSD, 4X memory
Disk seek 10,000,000 ns 10,000 us 10 ms 20x data center roundtrip
Read 1 MB sequentially from disk 20,000,000 ns 20,000 us 20 ms 80x memory, 20X SSD
Send packet CA->Netherlands->CA 150,000,000 ns 150,000 us 150 ms
Notes
-----
1 ns = 10^-9 seconds
1 us = 10^-6 seconds = 1,000 ns
1 ms = 10^-3 seconds = 1,000 us = 1,000,000 ns
Credit
------
By Jeff Dean: http://research.google.com/people/jeff/
Originally by Peter Norvig: http://norvig.com/21-days.html#answers
Contributions
-------------
Some updates from: https://gist.github.com/2843375
"Humanized" comparison: https://gist.github.com/2843375
Visual comparison chart: http://i.imgur.com/k0t1e.png
Animated presentation: http://prezi.com/pdkvgys-r0y6/latency-numbers-for-programmers-web-development/latency.txt
https://gist.github.com/jboner/2841832
https://gist.github.com/andrewscaya/2f9e68d4b41f9d747b92fb26b1b60d9f
```

It comes as no great surprise that reading from disk is always slower than memory and that network I/O calls remain the slowest of them all.

Let's delve a little deeper by having a look at some code that makes a series of I/O calls. Our first example will use cURL. Let's have a look at the following code:

```php
// chap4_IO_blocking.php

$start = microtime(true);

$i = 0;

$responses = [];
```

```
while ($i < 10) {

    $curl = curl_init();

    curl_setopt_array($curl, array(
        CURLOPT_RETURNTRANSFER => 1,
        CURLOPT_URL => 'http://www.google.ca',
        CURLOPT_USERAGENT => 'Faster Web cURL Request'
    ));

    $responses[] = curl_exec($curl);

    curl_close($curl);

    $i++;
}

$time = microtime(true) - $start;

echo 'Time elapsed: ' . $time . PHP_EOL;

echo memory_get_usage() . ' bytes' . PHP_EOL;
```

Now, let's execute the PHP script. We should now see the following results:

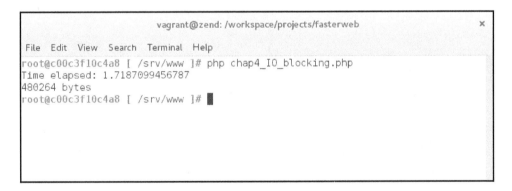

Time elapsed and memory consumed when running the blocking code script

This code takes a long time to complete because of the high latency associated with accessing the network.

If we profile the previous code using `Blackfire.io`, we can see that the 10 calls to cURL take over a second to complete:

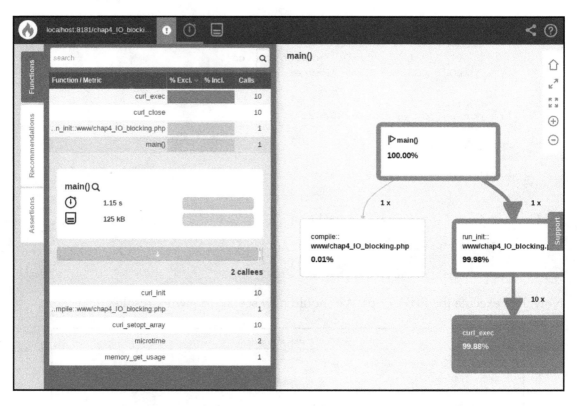

Profiling the code shows us that the 10 calls to cURL make up the greater part of the script's total execution time

Let's modify our PHP script in order to use asynchronous code to run our cURL requests simultaneously. Here is the new version of the previous PHP code:

```
// chap4_IO_non_blocking.php

$start = microtime(true);

$i = 0;

$curlHandles = [];

$responses = [];

$multiHandle = curl_multi_init();
```

```
for ($i = 0; $i < 10; $i++) {

    $curlHandles[$i] = curl_init();

    curl_setopt_array($curlHandles[$i], array(
        CURLOPT_RETURNTRANSFER => 1,
        CURLOPT_URL => 'http://www.google.ca',
        CURLOPT_USERAGENT => 'Faster Web cURL Request'
    ));

    curl_multi_add_handle($multiHandle, $curlHandles[$i]);
}

$running = null;

do {
    curl_multi_exec($multiHandle, $running);
} while ($running);

for ($i = 0; $i < 10; $i++) {
    curl_multi_remove_handle($multiHandle, $curlHandles[$i]);

    $responses[] = curl_multi_getcontent($curlHandles[$i]);
}

curl_multi_close($multiHandle);

$time = microtime(true) - $start;

echo 'Time elapsed: ' . $time . PHP_EOL;

echo memory_get_usage() . ' bytes' . PHP_EOL;
```

After executing the code, we now get the following results:

Time elapsed and memory consumed when running the non-blocking code script

As expected, the PHP script is faster as it no longer has to wait for the I/O calls to complete before continuing to execute the rest of the code. What is actually happening under the hood is multitasking within the same thread. The code's flow of execution is in fact interrupted in order to allow for concurrent execution of the many I/O calls. This is possible due to non-blocking code that will yield control back to the caller code while waiting for some task to complete, and possibly call a callback function when done. If we profile the previous code using `Blackfire.io`, we will see this looping in action—the yielding function is actually called more than 45,000 times in order to complete all 10 requests:

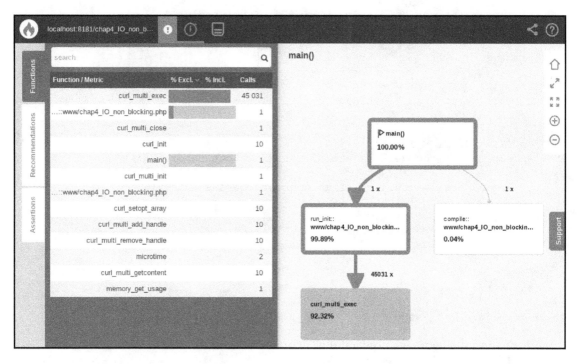

The yielding function is called more than 45,000 times in order to complete all 10 cURL requests

Introduced in PHP 5.5, generators allow for what seems to be simultaneous execution of different parts of the code and thus easier asynchronous programming. A generator is actually an invokable object that implements the iterator interface. The underlying principle is therefore to have a loop that will repeatedly call a generator function that will, in turn, yield control back to the loop until there is nothing left to process, in which case the generator function will return definitely.

Now, let's dig a little deeper into asynchronous programming with a simple code example. To do so, let's program a basic car race using the following code:

```php
// chap4_async_race.php

$laps[] = 0;
$laps[] = 0;
$laps[] = 0;

function car1(int &$lap) {
    while ($lap <= 10) {
        for ($x = 0; $x <= 200; $x++) {
            yield 0;
        }

        yield 1;
    }

    // If the car has finished its race, return null in order to remove the
car from the race
    return;
}

function car2(int &$lap) {
    while ($lap <= 10) {
        for ($x = 0; $x <= 220; $x++) {
            yield 0;
        }

        yield 1;
    }

    // If the car has finished its race, return null in order to remove the
car from the race
    return;
}

function car3(int &$lap) {
    while ($lap <= 10) {
        for ($x = 0; $x <= 230; $x++) {
            yield 0;
        }

        yield 1;
    }

    // If the car has finished its race, return null in order to remove the
```

```
car from the race
    return;
}

function runner(array $cars, array &$laps) {
    $flag = FALSE;

    while (TRUE) {
        foreach ($cars as $key => $car) {
            $penalty = rand(0, 8);
            if($key == $penalty) {
                // We must advance the car pointer in order to truly apply
the penalty
                                                                      to the
"current" car
                $car->next();
            } else {
                // Check if the "current" car pointer points to an active
race car
                if($car->current() !== NULL) {
                    // Check if the "current" car pointer points to a car
that has
completed a lap
                    if($car->current() == 1) {
                        $lapNumber = $laps[$key]++;
                        $carNumber = $key + 1;
                        if ($lapNumber == 10 && $flag === FALSE) {
                            echo "*** Car $carNumber IS THE WINNER! ***\n";
                            $flag = TRUE;
                        } else {
                            echo "Car $carNumber has completed lap
$lapNumber\n";
                        }
                    }
                    // Advance the car pointer
                    $car->next();
                    // If the next car is no longer active, remove the car
from the
race
                    if (!$car->valid()) {
                        unset($cars[$key]);
                    }
                }
            }
        }
    }
```

```
        // No active cars left! The race is over!
        if (empty($cars)) return;
    }
}

runner(array(car1($laps[0]), car2($laps[1]), car3($laps[2])), $laps);
```

As you can see, the runner function, which is the main loop, processes the three generator functions in random order until none of them have anything left to process. The end result is that we never know which car is going to win the race, although some of these cars seem to be going faster than others! Let's run this code three times. Here are the results for the first run:

```
                    vagrant@zend: /workspace/projects/fasterweb            ×

 File  Edit  View  Search  Terminal  Help
Car 1 has completed lap 3
Car 3 has completed lap 3
Car 2 has completed lap 4
Car 3 has completed lap 4
Car 2 has completed lap 5
Car 1 has completed lap 4
Car 3 has completed lap 5
Car 2 has completed lap 6
Car 3 has completed lap 6
Car 2 has completed lap 7
Car 1 has completed lap 5
Car 3 has completed lap 7
Car 2 has completed lap 8
Car 1 has completed lap 6
Car 3 has completed lap 8
Car 1 has completed lap 7
Car 2 has completed lap 9
Car 3 has completed lap 9
Car 1 has completed lap 8
*** Car 2 IS THE WINNER! ***
Car 3 has completed lap 10
Car 1 has completed lap 9
Car 1 has completed lap 10
root@c00c3f10c4a8 [ /srv/www ]#
```

Car 2 wins the race!

Here are the results for the second run:

```
vagrant@zend: /workspace/projects/fasterweb                    ×

File  Edit  View  Search  Terminal  Help
Car 2 has completed lap 3
Car 3 has completed lap 4
Car 1 has completed lap 3
Car 2 has completed lap 4
Car 3 has completed lap 5
Car 2 has completed lap 5
Car 1 has completed lap 4
Car 3 has completed lap 6
Car 2 has completed lap 6
Car 1 has completed lap 5
Car 3 has completed lap 7
Car 2 has completed lap 7
Car 3 has completed lap 8
Car 2 has completed lap 8
Car 1 has completed lap 6
Car 3 has completed lap 9
Car 1 has completed lap 7
Car 2 has completed lap 9
*** Car 3 IS THE WINNER! ***
Car 1 has completed lap 8
Car 2 has completed lap 10
Car 1 has completed lap 9
Car 1 has completed lap 10
root@c00c3f10c4a8 [ /srv/www ]#
```

Car 3 wins the race!

Here are the results for the third and final run:

```
                    vagrant@zend: /workspace/projects/fasterweb        x

 File  Edit  View  Search  Terminal  Help
Car 1 has completed lap 3
Car 2 has completed lap 3
Car 3 has completed lap 4
Car 1 has completed lap 4
Car 2 has completed lap 4
Car 3 has completed lap 5
Car 1 has completed lap 5
Car 2 has completed lap 5
Car 1 has completed lap 6
Car 3 has completed lap 6
Car 2 has completed lap 6
Car 1 has completed lap 7
Car 3 has completed lap 7
Car 2 has completed lap 7
Car 1 has completed lap 8
Car 3 has completed lap 8
Car 1 has completed lap 9
Car 2 has completed lap 8
Car 3 has completed lap 9
*** Car 1 IS THE WINNER! ***
Car 2 has completed lap 9
Car 3 has completed lap 10
Car 2 has completed lap 10
root@c00c3f10c4a8 [ /srv/www ]#
```

Car 1 wins the race!

The end result is what seems to be the simultaneous execution of three different functions within the same thread. This is what asynchronous programming is all about in its essential principle. Indeed, it is easy to understand how multitasking can, for example, be used to help mitigate the effects of a heavy workload on a single PHP script by interrupting the script's execution in order to queue some tasks using third-party software, like RabbitMQ and Redis. Thus, it becomes possible to delay the processing of these tasks until such time as processing is deemed appropriate.

Now that we have had a look at multitasking, let's have a look at multithreading.

Multithreading with pthreads

POSIX Threads, better known as pthreads, is a library that allows a computer program to execute multiple processes or threads concurrently by forking child processes from its parent process. The pthreads library can be used in PHP, making it therefore possible to fork processes in the background while executing something else simultaneously. Thus, multithreading is another way to cope with latency in I/O calls. In order to accomplish this, we will need a thread-safe version of PHP with the pthreads extension enabled. In our case, we will use a Linux for PHP container that is running a **Zend thread-safe (ZTS)** version of PHP 7.0.29. Open a new Terminal window, cd into the project's directory and enter the following command:

```
# docker run -it --rm \
> -p 8282:80 \
> -v ${PWD}/:/srv/fasterweb \
> asclinux/linuxforphp-8.1:7.0.29-zts \
> /bin/bash
```

Once you are done entering this command, you should see the following information if you enter the php -v command in the CLI:

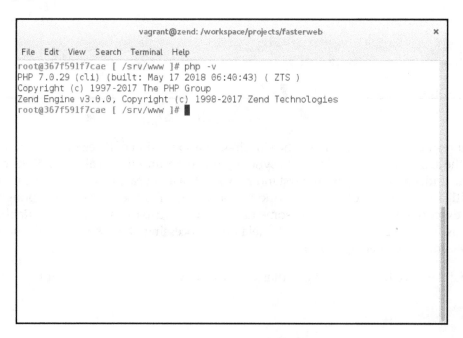

The ZTS container's command-line interface (CLI)

This message confirms we are using a thread-safe (ZTS) version of PHP. Then, on the container's CLI, enter these commands:

```
# mv /srv/www /srv/www.OLD
# ln -s /srv/fasterweb/chapter_4 /srv/www
# cd /srv/www
# pecl install pthreads
# echo "extension=pthreads.so" >> /etc/php.ini
```

You can now check that the pthreads extension is properly installed by entering the command php -i. The last command should allow you to see the extension's version number. If this is the case, then the extension was installed correctly:

```
vagrant@zend: /workspace/projects/fasterweb                              ×

 File  Edit  View  Search  Terminal  Help
Portions of tar implementation Copyright (c) 2003-2009 Tim Kientzle.
Directive => Local Value => Master Value
phar.cache_list => no value => no value
phar.readonly => On => On
phar.require_hash => On => On

posix

Revision => $Id: 771e31632526e20243748d73c150d8977fff1781 $

pthreads

Version => 3.1.6

readline

Readline Support => enabled
Readline library => 6.3

Directive => Local Value => Master Value
cli.pager => no value => no value
cli.prompt => \b \>  => \b \>

Reflection
```

Version 3.1.6 of the pthreads extension is now installed

Now that the `pthreads` library is installed and enabled, let's proceed to use it by trying to create multiple threads that will truly execute simultaneously on the computer's CPUs. To do so, we will use the following source code:

```php
// chap4_pthreads.php

$start = microtime(true);

class TestThreads extends Thread {

    protected $arg;

    public function __construct($arg) {
        $this->arg = $arg;
    }

    public function run() {
        if ($this->arg) {
            $sleep = mt_rand(1, 10);
            printf('%s: %s  -start -sleeps %d' . "\n", date("g:i:sa"),
$this->arg,
$sleep);
            sleep($sleep);
            printf('%s: %s  -finish' . "\n", date("g:i:sa"), $this->arg);
        }
    }
}

$stack = array();

// Create Multiple Thread
foreach ( range('1', '9') as $id ) {
    $stack[] = new TestThreads($id);
}

// Execute threads
foreach ( $stack as $thread ) {
    $thread->start();
}

sleep(1);

$time = microtime(true) - $start;

echo 'Time elapsed: ' . $time . PHP_EOL;

echo memory_get_usage() . ' bytes' . PHP_EOL;
```

Once executed, we obtain the following output:

```
                        vagrant@zend: /workspace/projects/fasterweb                    ×

 File  Edit  View  Search  Terminal  Help
root@c42690ecbc44 [ /srv/www ]# php chap4_pthreads.php
4:52:16am: 1   -start -sleeps 4
4:52:16am: 2   -start -sleeps 5
4:52:16am: 3   -start -sleeps 3
4:52:16am: 4   -start -sleeps 2
4:52:16am: 5   -start -sleeps 5
4:52:16am: 6   -start -sleeps 5
4:52:16am: 7   -start -sleeps 2
4:52:16am: 8   -start -sleeps 3
4:52:16am: 9   -start -sleeps 10
Time elapsed: 1.0299170017242
358248 bytes
4:52:18am: 4   -finish
4:52:18am: 7   -finish
4:52:19am: 3   -finish
4:52:19am: 8   -finish
4:52:20am: 1   -finish
4:52:21am: 2   -finish
4:52:21am: 5   -finish
4:52:21am: 6   -finish
4:52:26am: 9   -finish
root@c42690ecbc44 [ /srv/www ]# 
```

Threads were executed simultaneously

The results clearly show that the threads were executed simultaneously as the total elapsed time for the script was 10 seconds even though each thread slept for at least a few seconds. If this synchronous blocking code was executed without multithreading, it would have taken approximately 40 seconds in all to complete execution. Multitasking would not have been an appropriate solution in this case, as the blocking calls to the sleep() function would have prevented each generator from yielding control to the main loop.

Now that we have seen both multitasking via asynchronous programming and multithreading via the POSIX Threads library, we will turn our attention to a PHP library that can be very useful when it comes to programming asynchronously, namely the ReactPHP library.

Using the ReactPHP library

ReactPHP is an event-driven, non-blocking I/O library. This library relies essentially on an event loop that polls file descriptors, uses timers and defers callbacks by registering and executing outstanding ticks on each iteration of the loop.

ReactPHP is based on the Reactor pattern which, according to Douglas C. Schmidt, is a *"design pattern that handles service requests that are delivered concurrently to an application by one or more clients. Each service in an application may consist of several methods and is represented by a separate event handler that is responsible for dispatching service-specific requests. Dispatching of event handlers is performed by an initiation dispatcher, which manages the registered event handlers. Demultiplexing of service requests is performed by a synchronous event demultiplexer."* In Schmidt's original paper *Reactor: An Object Behavioral Pattern for Demultiplexing and Dispatching Handles for Synchronous Events*, we can find this UML representation of this pattern:

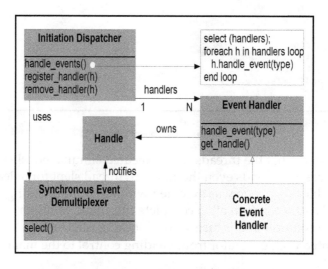

The Reactor pattern according to Douglas C. Schmidt

Let's start exploring this asynchronous programming library by installing it in our code repository. On the container's CLI, enter the following commands:

```
# cd /srv/www/react
# php composer.phar self-update
# php composer.phar install
# cd examples
```

Once the library is installed through Composer, you can try any of the example scripts that you can find in the examples directory. These code examples come from *ReactPHP*'s main code repository. In our case, we will start by having a look at the `parallel-download.php` script. Here is its source code:

```php
// parallel-download.php

$start = microtime(true);

// downloading the two best technologies ever in parallel

require __DIR__
    . DIRECTORY_SEPARATOR
    .'..'
    . DIRECTORY_SEPARATOR
    . 'vendor'
    . DIRECTORY_SEPARATOR
    .'autoload.php';

$loop = React\EventLoop\Factory::create();

$files = array(
    'node-v0.6.18.tar.gz' =>
'http://nodejs.org/dist/v0.6.18/node-v0.6.18.tar.gz',
    'php-5.5.15.tar.gz' =>
'http://it.php.net/get/php-5.5.15.tar.gz/from/this/mirror',
);

foreach ($files as $file => $url) {
    $readStream = fopen($url, 'r');
    $writeStream = fopen($file, 'w');

    stream_set_blocking($readStream, 0);
    stream_set_blocking($writeStream, 0);

    $read = new React\Stream\Stream($readStream, $loop);
    $write = new React\Stream\Stream($writeStream, $loop);

    $read->on('end', function () use ($file, &$files) {
        unset($files[$file]);
        echo "Finished downloading $file\n";
    });

    $read->pipe($write);

}
```

```php
$loop->addPeriodicTimer(5, function ($timer) use (&$files) {
    if (0 === count($files)) {
        $timer->cancel();
    }

    foreach ($files as $file => $url) {

        $mbytes = filesize($file) / (1024 * 1024);
        $formatted = number_format($mbytes, 3);
        echo "$file: $formatted MiB\n";
    }
});

echo "This script will show the download status every 5 seconds.\n";

$loop->run();

$time = microtime(true) - $start;

echo 'Time elapsed: ' . $time . PHP_EOL;

echo memory_get_usage() . ' bytes' . PHP_EOL;
```

Essentially, this script creates two streams, sets them to the non-blocking mode and registers the streams with the loop. A timer is added to the loop in order to echo a message every 5 seconds. Finally, it runs the loop.

Let's have a look at this script in action using the following command:

```
# php parallel-download.php
```

Here are the results:

```
File  Edit  View  Search  Terminal  Help
root@c42690ecbc44 [ /srv/www/react/examples ]# php parallel-download.php
This script will show the download status every 5 seconds.
node-v0.6.18.tar.gz: 5.891 MiB
php-5.5.15.tar.gz: 1.118 MiB
Finished downloading node-v0.6.18.tar.gz
php-5.5.15.tar.gz: 1.118 MiB
php-5.5.15.tar.gz: 1.118 MiB
Finished downloading php-5.5.15.tar.gz
Time elapsed: 20.972438097
926784 bytes
root@c42690ecbc44 [ /srv/www/react/examples ]# █
```

The two packages are downloaded asynchronously

As you can see, the downloads were executed in a parallel, asynchronous and reactive way.

Let's continue our short journey into the world of ReactPHP by having a little bit of fun with the `tcp-chat.php` script that is included in the code examples. Here is the source code of this code example:

```php
// tcp-chat.php

// socket based chat

require __DIR__
    . DIRECTORY_SEPARATOR
    .'..'
    . DIRECTORY_SEPARATOR
    . 'vendor'
    . DIRECTORY_SEPARATOR
    .'autoload.php';

$loop = React\EventLoop\Factory::create();
$socket = new React\Socket\Server($loop);

$conns = new \SplObjectStorage();

$socket->on('connection', function ($conn) use ($conns) {
    $conns->attach($conn);
```

```
$conn->on('data', function ($data) use ($conns, $conn) {
    foreach ($conns as $current) {

        if ($conn === $current) {
            continue;
        }

        $current->write($conn->getRemoteAddress().': ');
        $current->write($data);
    }

});

$conn->on('end', function () use ($conns, $conn) {
    $conns->detach($conn);
});
});

echo "Socket server listening on port 4000.\n";
echo "You can connect to it by running: telnet localhost 4000\n";

$socket->listen(4000);
$loop->run();
```

The script creates a socket server that listens on port 4000 and is informed by the loop of incoming connections by listening for a connection event. Upon notification of the event, the socket server injects the connection object into the handler. The connection object then starts listening for the data event which will trigger it to do something with the data received from the socket server's client. In the case of this chat script, the connection object will trigger the write methods of all registered connection objects found in the SplObjectStorage object, thus effectively sending the message to all currently connected chat clients.

First, start the chat server by running the script:

```
# php tcp-chat.php
```

Then, open three new Terminal windows and connect to our *Linux for PHP Docker* container by entering the following commands in each window:

```
# docker exec -it $( docker ps -q | awk '{ print $1 }' ) /bin/bash
```

On each container's CLI, enter the following command:

```
# telnet localhost 4000
```

Once connected through `telnet`, just have fun sending messages back and forth from one Terminal window to the other:

```
                        vagrant@zend: ~                          ×
  File  Edit  View  Search  Terminal  Help
 Trying 127.0.0.1...
 Connected to localhost.
 Escape character is '^]'.
 127.0.0.1: Hello?
 Hi from window no 1!
 127.0.0.1: Hi from window no 2!
 127.0.0.1: Hi from window no 3!

                        vagrant@zend: ~                          ×
  File  Edit  View  Search  Terminal  Help
 Trying 127.0.0.1...
 Connected to localhost.
 Escape character is '^]'.
 127.0.0.1: Hello?
 127.0.0.1: Hi from window no 1!
 Hi from window no 2!
 127.0.0.1: Hi from window no 3!

                        vagrant@zend: ~                          ×
  File  Edit  View  Search  Terminal  Help
 Trying 127.0.0.1...
 Connected to localhost.
 Escape character is '^]'.
 Hello?
 127.0.0.1: Hi from window no 1!
 127.0.0.1: Hi from window no 2!
 Hi from window no 3!
```

Sending messages from one terminal window to the others

Obviously, what has been done here using Terminal windows within the same container could have been done using Terminal windows on different computers through networking. This example shows us just how powerful asynchronous programming can be.

Let's complete our survey of *ReactPHP*'s code examples by having a look at the `scalability.php` script. Here is its source code:

```
// scalability.php

// a simple, single-process, horizontal scalable http server listening on
10 ports
```

```
require __DIR__
    . DIRECTORY_SEPARATOR
    .'..'
    . DIRECTORY_SEPARATOR
    . 'vendor'
    . DIRECTORY_SEPARATOR
    .'autoload.php';

$loop = React\EventLoop\Factory::create();

for ($i = 0; $i < 10; ++$i) {

    $s = stream_socket_server('tcp://127.0.0.1:' . (8000 + $i));
    $loop->addReadStream($s, function ($s) use ($i) {
        $c = stream_socket_accept($s);
        $len = strlen($i) + 4;
        fwrite($c,"HTTP/1.1 200 OK\r\nContent-Length:
$len\r\n\r\nHi:$i\n");
        echo "Served on port 800$i\n";
    });

}

echo "Access your brand new HTTP server on 127.0.0.1:800x. Replace x with
any number from 0-9\n";

$loop->run();
```

The script creates a socket server which is then attached to the main event loop in order to call a lambda function when a request is sent to the server. The lambda function then executes the code that will send the answer back to the client by writing it to the accepted stream socket.

Let's run this code with the following command:

```
# php scalability.php
```

Then, open another Terminal window and connect it to our *Linux for PHP Docker* container:

```
# docker exec -it $( docker ps -q | awk '{ print $1 }' ) /bin/bash
```

Then, query the server using wget:

```
# wget -nv -O - http://localhost:8000
# wget -nv -O - http://localhost:8001
# wget -nv -O - http://localhost:8002
# wget -nv -O - http://localhost:8003
```

```
# wget -nv -O - http://localhost:8004
# wget -nv -O - http://localhost:8005
# wget -nv -O - http://localhost:8006
# wget -nv -O - http://localhost:8007
# wget -nv -O - http://localhost:8008
# wget -nv -O - http://localhost:8009
```

Once done, you should get the following responses for each request:

```
                              vagrant@zend: ~                                    ×

 File  Edit  View  Search  Terminal  Help
root@6c9d0310ab84 [ / ]# wget -nv -O - http://localhost:8000
Hi:0
2017-12-28 21:47:13 URL:http://localhost:8000/ [5/5] -> "-" [1]
root@6c9d0310ab84 [ / ]# wget -nv -O - http://localhost:8001
Hi:1
2017-12-28 21:47:17 URL:http://localhost:8001/ [5/5] -> "-" [1]
root@6c9d0310ab84 [ / ]# wget -nv -O - http://localhost:8002
Hi:2
2017-12-28 21:47:18 URL:http://localhost:8002/ [5/5] -> "-" [1]
root@6c9d0310ab84 [ / ]# wget -nv -O - http://localhost:8003
Hi:3
2017-12-28 21:47:20 URL:http://localhost:8003/ [5/5] -> "-" [1]
root@6c9d0310ab84 [ / ]# wget -nv -O - http://localhost:8004
Hi:4
2017-12-28 21:47:21 URL:http://localhost:8004/ [5/5] -> "-" [1]
root@6c9d0310ab84 [ / ]# wget -nv -O - http://localhost:8005
Hi:5
2017-12-28 21:47:23 URL:http://localhost:8005/ [5/5] -> "-" [1]
root@6c9d0310ab84 [ / ]# wget -nv -O - http://localhost:8006
Hi:6
2017-12-28 21:47:26 URL:http://localhost:8006/ [5/5] -> "-" [1]
root@6c9d0310ab84 [ / ]# wget -nv -O - http://localhost:8007
Hi:7
2017-12-28 21:47:52 URL:http://localhost:8007/ [5/5] -> "-" [1]
root@6c9d0310ab84 [ / ]# wget -nv -O - http://localhost:8008
Hi:8
2017-12-28 21:47:55 URL:http://localhost:8008/ [5/5] -> "-" [1]
root@6c9d0310ab84 [ / ]# wget -nv -O - http://localhost:8009
Hi:9
2017-12-28 21:47:57 URL:http://localhost:8009/ [5/5] -> "-" [1]
root@6c9d0310ab84 [ / ]#
```

Connecting to each available port of the web server

This is what you should see on the server side:

```
                    vagrant@zend: /workspace/projects/fasterweb                    ×

  File  Edit  View  Search  Terminal  Help
root@6c9d0310ab84 [ /srv/www/react/examples ]# php scalability.php
Access your brand new HTTP server on 127.0.0.1:800x. Replace x with any number f
rom 0-9
Served on port 8000
Served on port 8001
Served on port 8002
Served on port 8003
Served on port 8004
Served on port 8005
Served on port 8006
Served on port 8007
Served on port 8008
Served on port 8009
```

The server confirms having served all these requests on all these ports

Again, you can see how powerful *ReactPHP* can be, as only a few lines of code are enough to create a scalable web server.

Moreover, we highly recommend that all the files from the *ReactPHP* project that are included in our repository be explored and tried out so you can fully appreciate what this library can do for you as a developer when it comes to asynchronous programming.

Also, there are other great asynchronous PHP libraries that can help you as you master this new way to develop and speed up high latency I/O applications. One such library is *Amp* (https://amphp.org/). It is well worth the time to explore these very useful libraries while mastering the art of asynchronous programming.

Finally, for more information on asynchronous programming in PHP, you can listen to a great presentation given on this topic by *Christopher Pitt* at *Nomad PHP* (https://nomadphp.com/asynchronous-php/).

Summary

In this chapter, we have learned how to determine the best strategies to cope with I/O calls and how to implement these strategies. Moreover, we have seen how to use the ReactPHP library and how to benefit from event-driven programming when dealing with asynchronous I/O calls.

In the next chapter, we will learn how to measure database performance, ranging from applying simple measurement techniques to using advanced benchmarking tools.

5
Measuring and Optimizing Database Performance

In the first chapter of this book, we used the `mysqlslap` tool to learn how to do basic MySQL benchmarking. In this chapter, we will use this tool and others to do more advanced benchmarking with our MariaDB (MySQL) server. But, first, we will learn query optimization techniques that will use some of MySQL's built-in features in order to better analyze our SQL queries.

Thus, we will learn how to measure and optimize database performance through the use of simple measurement techniques such as query optimization. Also, we will see how to use advanced database benchmarking tools, such as **DBT2** and **SysBench**.

Therefore, we will cover the following points:

- Measuring and optimizing SQL query performance
- Installing, configuring and using advanced database benchmarking tools

SQL query performance

In order to better understand SQL query performance, we must first understand what indexes are and how they are built.

The structure of indexes

An index is an ordered list of table elements. These elements are first stored in a physically unordered doubly linked list. The list is doubly linked to the table through pointers to the table entries and to a second structure that stores the index values in a logical order, a balanced tree or b-tree. Thus, indexes have an algorithmic complexity that is logarithmic—$O(\log n)$—for read operations on average, which means that the database engine should maintain speed even if there is a significant number of entries in the table. Indeed, an index lookup implies three steps:

- The tree traversal
- Searching the leaf node chain
- Fetching the data from the table

Thus, an index lookup is great when reading from the b-tree only, as you avoid the linear—$O(n)$—full table scan, for example. That being said though, you can never avoid the overhead complexity caused by keeping the index up to date when writing to the table.

This brings us to our first consideration about query optimization: what is the final purpose of the table's data? Are we simply logging information or are we storing a user's shopping cart items? Are we querying a table that is mostly read from or written to? This is important, as optimizing one SELECT query might slow down a whole series of other INSERT or UPDATE queries to the same table.

A second consideration would be the nature of the table's data. Are we trying to index values that generate equivocity for example, thus forcing the database engine to do further lookups in the leaf nodes of the b-tree in order to determine all the values that truly fulfill the expectations of a specific query? When equivocity is an issue, we might end up with a "slow index" or what is often called the "degenerated index".

A third consideration is the economy of efficiency surrounding the act of querying the table. How powerful is the underlying computer? How many users are querying the table at a given time on average? Is scalability important?

One last consideration is the storage size of the data. It is important to know that, as a general rule, indexes grow, on average, to about 10% of the original table's size. Therefore, when tables are large in size, it is expected that the table's indexes will be bigger in size also. And, of course, the bigger the index, the longer you will be waiting due to I/O latency.

These considerations will determine which query to optimize and how to optimize it. Sometimes, optimizing is doing nothing.

Now that we better understand indexes, let's start analyzing simple SQL queries in order to understand database engine execution plans.

The execution plan

We will begin understanding the execution plan by analyzing simple WHERE clauses. To do so, we will use our first Linux for PHP Docker container. In the first chapter, we loaded the Sakila database into the MariaDB (MySQL) server. We will now use it to learn how an execution plan works and when to use query optimization techniques. Once on the container's CLI, enter the following commands:

```
# mysql -uroot
# MariaDB > USE sakila;
# MariaDB > SELECT * FROM actor WHERE first_name = 'AL';
```

These commands should yield the following results:

```
                          vagrant@zend: /workspace/projects/fasterweb                    ×

 File  Edit  View  Search  Terminal  Help
root@7fffa5541d43 [ / ]# mysql -uroot
Welcome to the MariaDB monitor.  Commands end with ; or \g.
Your MariaDB connection id is 12
Server version: 10.2.8-MariaDB Source distribution

Copyright (c) 2000, 2017, Oracle, MariaDB Corporation Ab and others.

Type 'help;' or '\h' for help. Type '\c' to clear the current input statement.

MariaDB [(none)]> use sakila;
Database changed
MariaDB [sakila]> SELECT * FROM actor WHERE first_name = 'AL';
+----------+------------+-----------+---------------------+
| actor_id | first_name | last_name | last_update         |
+----------+------------+-----------+---------------------+
|      165 | AL         | GARLAND   | 2006-02-15 04:34:33 |
+----------+------------+-----------+---------------------+
1 row in set (0.00 sec)

MariaDB [sakila]> █
```

The result of the SELECT statement

At first glance, this query seems to be fine with an execution time of 0.00 seconds. But, is this truly the case? To further analyze this query, we will have to have a look at the database engine's execution plan. To do so, enter the keyword EXPLAIN at the beginning of the query:

```
# MariaDB > EXPLAIN SELECT * FROM actor WHERE first_name = 'AL';
```

The following results give us some information on the execution plan:

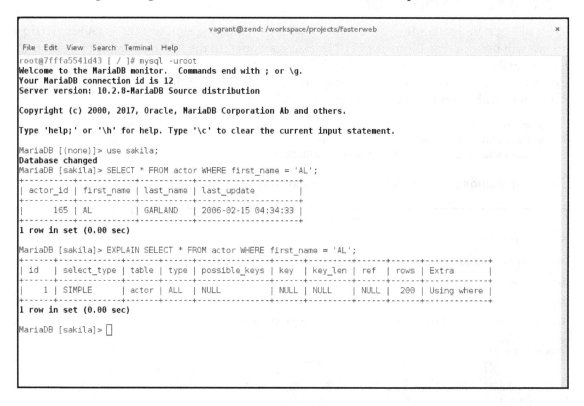

The execution plan of the same SELECT statement

Let's take the time to define each column of this result set:

- The id column tells us in what order tables were joined. In this case, there is only one table.
- The select_type is SIMPLE, which means that there were no subqueries, unions, or dependent query types done to execute this query.

- The `table` column gives us the name of the table that was the object of the query. If it had been a temporary materialized table, we would have seen the expression `<subquery#>` in this column.
- The `type` column is very important for query optimization. It gives us information on table access and how rows are found and retrieved from the table. In this case, a red flag is raised because we can see that the value of this column is `ALL`. To read further on the different possible values of this very important column, please consult the MariaDB manual at `https://mariadb.com/kb/en/library/explain/`.
- The `possible_keys` column informs us of keys in the table that could be used to answer the query. In this example, the value is `NULL`.
- The `key` column indicates the key that was actually used. Here, again, the value is `NULL`.
- A value in the `key_len` column would mean that only a certain number of bytes of a multi-column key was used to complete the query lookup.
- The `ref` column tells us which columns or constants are used to compare against the used index. Of course, since no index was used to execute this query, the value of this column is `NULL` also.
- The `rows` column indicates the number of rows the database engine will have to examine in order to complete its execution plan. In this example, the engine has to go through the 200 rows. If the table was large and had to be joined to a previous table, performance would drop fairly quickly.
- The last column is the `Extra` column. This column will give us more information on the execution plan. In this example, the database engine uses the `WHERE` clause as it has to do a full table scan.

Basic query optimization

In order to start optimizing this query, we must go through what I have called previously *initial considerations* of query optimization. For the sake of this example, let's say that this table will be the object of `READ` queries more than `WRITE` queries because the data will remain fairly static once written to the table. Also, it is important to note that creating an index on the `first_name` column of the `actor` table will make the index prone to generating equivocity due to non-unique values in this column. Moreover, let's say that scalability is important because we intend on having many users querying this table every hour and that the table size should remain manageable on a long-term period.

This being given and known, we will therefore proceed to create an index on the first_name column of the actor table:

 # MariaDB > CREATE INDEX idx_first_name ON actor(first_name);

Once done, MariaDB confirms the creation of the index:

```
MariaDB [sakila]> CREATE INDEX idx_first_name ON actor(first_name);
Query OK, 0 rows affected (0.14 sec)
Records: 0  Duplicates: 0  Warnings: 0
```

Confirmation that the index was created

Now that the index has been created, we obtain this result when asking the database engine to EXPLAIN its execution plan:

```
                              vagrant@zend: /workspace/projects/fasterweb                        x

 File  Edit  View  Search  Terminal  Help

MariaDB [(none)]> use sakila;
Database changed
MariaDB [sakila]> SELECT * FROM actor WHERE first_name = 'AL';
+----------+------------+-----------+---------------------+
| actor_id | first_name | last_name | last_update         |
+----------+------------+-----------+---------------------+
|      165 | AL         | GARLAND   | 2006-02-15 04:34:33 |
+----------+------------+-----------+---------------------+
1 row in set (0.00 sec)

MariaDB [sakila]> EXPLAIN SELECT * FROM actor WHERE first_name = 'AL';
+------+-------------+-------+------+---------------+------+---------+------+------+-------------+
| id   | select_type | table | type | possible_keys | key  | key_len | ref  | rows | Extra       |
+------+-------------+-------+------+---------------+------+---------+------+------+-------------+
|    1 | SIMPLE      | actor | ALL  | NULL          | NULL | NULL    | NULL |  200 | Using where |
+------+-------------+-------+------+---------------+------+---------+------+------+-------------+
1 row in set (0.00 sec)

MariaDB [sakila]> CREATE INDEX idx_first_name ON actor(first_name);
Query OK, 0 rows affected (0.14 sec)
Records: 0  Duplicates: 0  Warnings: 0

MariaDB [sakila]> EXPLAIN SELECT * FROM actor WHERE first_name = 'AL';
+------+-------------+-------+------+----------------+----------------+---------+-------+------+----------------
-------+
| id   | select_type | table | type | possible_keys  | key            | key_len | ref   | rows | Extra
       |
+------+-------------+-------+------+----------------+----------------+---------+-------+------+----------------
-------+
|    1 | SIMPLE      | actor | ref  | idx_first_name | idx_first_name | 137     | const |    1 | Using index con
dition |
+------+-------------+-------+------+----------------+----------------+---------+-------+------+----------------
-------+
1 row in set (0.00 sec)

MariaDB [sakila]> █
```

The execution plan is now optimized

The `type` column's value is now `ref`, `possible_keys` is `idx_first_name`, `key` is `idx_first_name`, `ref` is `const`, `rows` is 1 and `Extra` is `Using index condition`. As we can see, the engine has now identified our newly created index as a possible key to use and then proceeds to use it. It uses the constant value given in our query to perform the lookup in the index and considers only one row when accessing the table. All of this is great but, as we expected in our initial considerations, the index is composed of non-unique values. The possible equivocity amongst values of the table column might lead to a degenerated index over time, hence the access type of `ref` and the extra information indicating that the engine is `Using index condition`, which means that the `WHERE` clause is pushed down to the table engine for optimization at the index level. In this example, with the admitted initial considerations, this is, in the absolute sense, the best query optimization that we can do, as it is impossible to get unique values in the `first_name` column of the actor table. But, in fact, there is a possible optimization depending on the domain use case. If we only wish to use the actor's first name, then we could further optimize the `Using index condition` in the `Extra` column by only selecting the appropriate column, thus allowing the database engine to only access the index:

```
# MariaDB > EXPLAIN SELECT first_name FROM actor WHERE first_name = 'AL';
```

The database engine then confirms that it is only using the index in the `Extra` column:

```
MariaDB [sakila]> EXPLAIN SELECT first_name FROM actor WHERE first_name = 'AL';
+------+-------------+-------+------+---------------+---------------+---------+-------+------+----------------
----------+
| id   | select_type | table | type | possible_keys | key           | key_len | ref   | rows | Extra
       |
+------+-------------+-------+------+---------------+---------------+---------+-------+------+----------------
----------+
|    1 | SIMPLE      | actor | ref  | idx_first_name | idx_first_name | 137     | const |    1 | Using where; Us
ing index |
+------+-------------+-------+------+---------------+---------------+---------+-------+------+----------------
----------+
1 row in set (0.00 sec)

MariaDB [sakila]> []
```

The 'Extra' column now contains the information "Using where; Using index"

And, how does all of this translate into overall performance? Let's run a few benchmark tests in order to measure the effects of our changes.

First, we will run a benchmark test without the index. On the container's CLI, run the following command:

```
# mysqlslap --user=root --host=localhost --concurrency=1000 --number-of-
queries=10000 --create-schema=sakila --query="SELECT * FROM actor WHERE
first_name = 'AL';" --delimiter=";" --verbose --iterations=2 --debug-info;
```

Here are the results without the index:

```
                        vagrant@zend: /workspace/projects/fasterweb              ×

 File  Edit  View  Search  Terminal  Help
root@7fffa5541d43 [ / ]# mysqlslap --user=root --host=localhost --concurrency=10
00 --number-of-queries=10000 --create-schema=sakila --query="SELECT * FROM actor
 WHERE first_name = 'AL';" --delimiter=";" --verbose --iterations=2 --debug-info
Benchmark
        Average number of seconds to run all queries: 0.746 seconds
        Minimum number of seconds to run all queries: 0.741 seconds
        Maximum number of seconds to run all queries: 0.752 seconds
        Number of clients running queries: 1000
        Average number of queries per client: 10


User time 0.16, System time 0.38
Maximum resident set size 22032, Integral resident set size 0
Non-physical pagefaults 15627, Physical pagefaults 0, Swaps 0
Blocks in 0 out 0, Messages in 0 out 0, Signals 0
Voluntary context switches 46892, Involuntary context switches 775
root@7fffa5541d43 [ / ]# █
```

The results of the benchmark test WITHOUT the use of the index

And, the results with the index:

```
                        vagrant@zend: /workspace/projects/fasterweb              ×

 File  Edit  View  Search  Terminal  Help
root@7fffa5541d43 [ / ]# mysqlslap --user=root --host=localhost --concurrency=10
00 --number-of-queries=10000 --create-schema=sakila --query="SELECT * FROM actor
 WHERE first_name = 'AL';" --delimiter=";" --verbose --iterations=2 --debug-info
Benchmark
        Average number of seconds to run all queries: 0.655 seconds
        Minimum number of seconds to run all queries: 0.589 seconds
        Maximum number of seconds to run all queries: 0.722 seconds
        Number of clients running queries: 1000
        Average number of queries per client: 10


User time 0.12, System time 0.37
Maximum resident set size 22796, Integral resident set size 0
Non-physical pagefaults 15075, Physical pagefaults 0, Swaps 0
Blocks in 0 out 0, Messages in 0 out 0, Signals 0
Voluntary context switches 43223, Involuntary context switches 741
root@7fffa5541d43 [ / ]# █
```

The results of the benchmark test WITH the use of the index

And, finally, let's run the same command while only selecting the appropriate column, thus limiting the lookup to the index only:

```
# mysqlslap --user=root --host=localhost --concurrency=1000 --number-of-
queries=10000 --create-schema=sakila --query="SELECT first_name FROM actor
WHERE first_name = 'AL';" --delimiter=";" --verbose --iterations=2 --debug-
info;
```

Here are the results of this last benchmark test:

```
vagrant@zend: /workspace/projects/fasterweb                    ×

 File  Edit  View  Search  Terminal  Help
root@7fffa5541d43 [ / ]# mysqlslap --user=root --host=localhost --concurrency=10
00 --number-of-queries=10000 --create-schema=sakila --query="SELECT first_name F
ROM actor WHERE first_name = 'AL';" --delimiter=";" --verbose --iterations=2 --d
ebug-info
Benchmark
        Average number of seconds to run all queries: 0.539 seconds
        Minimum number of seconds to run all queries: 0.472 seconds
        Maximum number of seconds to run all queries: 0.606 seconds
        Number of clients running queries: 1000
        Average number of queries per client: 10


User time 0.14, System time 0.29
Maximum resident set size 24872, Integral resident set size 0
Non-physical pagefaults 15940, Physical pagefaults 0, Swaps 0
Blocks in 0 out 0, Messages in 0 out 0, Signals 0
Voluntary context switches 37897, Involuntary context switches 6211
root@7fffa5541d43 [ / ]# █
```

The results of the benchmark test WITH the use of the index ONLY

The benchmark test results clearly show that our query optimization did indeed satisfy our initial scalability assumption, especially if we were to see the table grow in size and our database become more popular with a growing number of users over time.

The performance schema and advanced query optimization

The art of query optimization can be pushed a little further still by using MariaDB's (MySQL) performance schema to profile queries. Query profiling allows us to see what is happening under the hood and to further optimize complex queries.

To begin, let's enable the performance schema on our database server. To do so, enter these commands on the Linux for PHP container's CLI:

```
# sed -i '/myisam_sort_buffer_size =/a performance_schema = ON'
/etc/mysql/my.cnf
# sed -i '/performance_schema =/a performance-schema-instrument =
"stage/%=ON"' /etc/mysql/my.cnf
# sed -i '/performance-schema-instrument =/a performance-schema-consumer-
events-stages-current = ON' /etc/mysql/my.cnf
# sed -i '/performance-schema-consumer-events-stages-current =/a
performance-schema-consumer-events-stages-history = ON' /etc/mysql/my.cnf
# sed -i '/performance-schema-consumer-events-stages-history =/a
performance-schema-consumer-events-stages-history-long = ON'
/etc/mysql/my.cnf
# /etc/init.d/mysql restart
# mysql -uroot
# MariaDB > USE performance_schema;
# MariaDB > UPDATE setup_instruments SET ENABLED = 'YES', TIMED = 'YES';
# MariaDB > UPDATE setup_consumers SET ENABLED = 'YES';
```

The database engine will confirm that some rows were modified in the performance_schema database:

```
MariaDB [performance_schema]> UPDATE setup_instruments SET ENABLED = 'YES', TIMED = 'YES';
Query OK, 293 rows affected (0.01 sec)
Rows matched: 676  Changed: 293  Warnings: 0

MariaDB [performance_schema]> UPDATE setup_consumers SET ENABLED = 'YES';
Query OK, 5 rows affected (0.00 sec)
Rows matched: 12  Changed: 5  Warnings: 0
```

The 'performance_schema' database has been modified

We can now check that the performance schema is now enabled:

```
# MariaDB > SHOW VARIABLES LIKE 'performance_schema';
```

The database engine should return the following result:

```
MariaDB [sakila]> SHOW VARIABLES LIKE 'performance_schema';
+--------------------+-------+
| Variable_name      | Value |
+--------------------+-------+
| performance_schema | ON    |
+--------------------+-------+
1 row in set (0.00 sec)
```

Confirmation that the performance schema is now enabled

Now that profiling is enabled and ready, let's run a complex query on the Sakila database. Using subqueries with the NOT IN clause often forces the engine to iteratively make an extra check against the main query. These queries can be optimized using JOIN statements. We will take the following query and run it on our database server:

```
# MariaDB > SELECT film.film_id
          > FROM film
          > WHERE film.rating = 'G'
          > AND film.film_id NOT IN (
               > SELECT film.film_id
               > FROM rental
               > LEFT JOIN inventory ON rental.inventory_id =
inventory.inventory_id
               > LEFT JOIN film ON inventory.film_id = film.film_id
          > );
```

Running the query yields the following result:

```
MariaDB [sakila]> SELECT film.film_id
    -> FROM film
    -> WHERE film.rating = 'G'
    -> AND film.film_id NOT IN (
    -> SELECT film.film_id
    -> FROM rental
    -> LEFT JOIN inventory ON rental.inventory_id = inventory.inventory_id
    -> LEFT JOIN film ON inventory.film_id = film.film_id
    -> );
+---------+
| film_id |
+---------+
|     128 |
|     217 |
|     318 |
|     419 |
|     497 |
|     860 |
|     954 |
+---------+
7 rows in set (0.02 sec)

MariaDB [sakila]> 
```

The result of the SELECT statement

And, here are the results when using the EXPLAIN statement on the previous query:

```
MariaDB [sakila]> EXPLAIN SELECT film.film_id FROM film WHERE film.rating = 'G' AND film.film_id NOT IN ( SELECT
 film.film_id FROM rental LEFT JOIN inventory ON rental.inventory_id = inventory.inventory_id LEFT JOIN film ON
inventory.film_id = film.film_id );
+------+--------------+-----------+--------+---------------+------------------+---------+----------------------
--------+------+-------------------------+
| id   | select_type  | table     | type   | possible_keys | key              | key_len | ref
      | rows | Extra                   |
+------+--------------+-----------+--------+---------------+------------------+---------+----------------------
--------+------+-------------------------+
|    1 | PRIMARY      | film      | ALL    | NULL          | NULL             | NULL    | NULL
      | 1000 | Using where             |
|    2 | MATERIALIZED | rental    | index  | NULL          | idx_fk_inventory_id | 3    | NULL
      | 16008 | Using index            |
|    2 | MATERIALIZED | inventory | eq_ref | PRIMARY       | PRIMARY          | 3       | sakila.rental.inven
tory_id |    1 |                         |
|    2 | MATERIALIZED | film      | eq_ref | PRIMARY       | PRIMARY          | 2       | sakila.inventory.fi
lm_id |      1 | Using where; Using index |
+------+--------------+-----------+--------+---------------+------------------+---------+----------------------
--------+------+-------------------------+
4 rows in set (0.00 sec)

MariaDB [sakila]>
```

The execution plan of the same SELECT statement

As we can see, the engine is doing a full table scan and uses a materialized subquery to complete its lookup. To see what is happening under the hood, we will have to see what events the profiler has recorded concerning this query. To do so, enter the following query:

```
# MariaDB > SELECT EVENT_ID, TRUNCATE(TIMER_WAIT/1000000000000, 6) as
Duration, SQL_TEXT
         > FROM performance_schema.events_statements_history_long WHERE
SQL_TEXT like
              '%NOT IN%';
```

Once this query is run, you will obtain the original query's unique identifier:

```
MariaDB [performance_schema]> SELECT EVENT_ID, TRUNCATE(TIMER_WAIT/1000000000000,6) as Duration, SQL_TEXT
 FROM performance_schema.events_statements_history_long WHERE SQL_TEXT like '%NOT IN%';
+----------+----------+-------------------------------------------
-----------------------------------------+
| EVENT_ID | Duration | SQL_TEXT
                                          |
+----------+----------+-------------------------------------------
-----------------------------------------+
|       43 | 0.015535 | SELECT film.film_id
FROM film
WHERE film.rating = 'G'
AND film.film_id NOT IN (
SELECT film.film_id
FROM rental
LEFT JOIN inventory ON rental.inventory_id = inventory.inventory_id
LEFT JOIN film ON inventory.film_id = film.film_id
) |
+----------+----------+-------------------------------------------
-----------------------------------------+
1 row in set (0.00 sec)
```

The original query's identifier

This information allows us to run the following query in order to get the list of the underlying events that took place when we ran our original query:

```
# MariaDB > SELECT event_name AS Stage,
TRUNCATE(TIMER_WAIT/1000000000000,6) AS Duration
        > FROM performance_schema.events_stages_history_long WHERE
NESTING_EVENT_ID=43;
```

Here is what we find in MariaDB's performance schema concerning our original query:

```
                           vagrant@zend: /workspace/projects/fasterweb                              ×

 File  Edit  View  Search  Terminal  Help
MariaDB [performance_schema]> SELECT event_name AS Stage, TRUNCATE(TIMER_WAIT/1000000000000,6) AS Duration
  FROM performance_schema.events_stages_history_long WHERE NESTING_EVENT_ID=43;
+-----------------------------------+----------+
| Stage                             | Duration |
+-----------------------------------+----------+
| stage/sql/init                    | 0.000165 |
| stage/sql/checking permissions    | 0.000001 |
| stage/sql/checking permissions    | 0.000000 |
| stage/sql/checking permissions    | 0.000000 |
| stage/sql/checking permissions    | 0.000019 |
| stage/sql/Opening tables          | 0.000122 |
| stage/sql/After opening tables    | 0.000000 |
| stage/sql/System lock             | 0.000014 |
| stage/sql/Table lock              | 0.000000 |
| stage/sql/init                    | 0.000109 |
| stage/sql/optimizing              | 0.000010 |
| stage/sql/statistics              | 0.000039 |
| stage/sql/preparing               | 0.000018 |
| stage/sql/optimizing              | 0.000005 |
| stage/sql/statistics              | 0.000136 |
| stage/sql/preparing               | 0.000053 |
| stage/sql/executing               | 0.000000 |
| stage/sql/Sending data            | 0.000216 |
| stage/sql/executing               | 0.000000 |
| stage/sql/Sending data            | 0.014527 |
| stage/sql/end                     | 0.000003 |
| stage/sql/query end               | 0.000005 |
| stage/sql/closing tables          | 0.000000 |
| stage/sql/Unlocking tables        | 0.000019 |
| stage/sql/freeing items           | 0.000002 |
| stage/sql/removing tmp table      | 0.000003 |
| stage/sql/removing tmp table      | 0.000000 |
| stage/sql/cleaning up             | 0.000000 |
+-----------------------------------+----------+
28 rows in set (0.00 sec)

MariaDB [performance_schema]> 
```

The query's profile reveals one particularly long operation

This result shows that the NOT IN clause caused the database engine to create a materialized subquery, as the inner query was optimized as a semi-join subquery. Thus, the engine had to do a few optimization operations before running the query and the materialized subquery. Moreover, the result shows that the materialized subquery was the most costly operation.

The easiest way to optimize these subqueries is to replace them with proper `JOIN` statements in the main query, as follows:

```
# MariaDB > SELECT film.film_id
#         > FROM rental
#         > INNER JOIN inventory ON rental.inventory_id =
inventory.inventory_id
#         > RIGHT JOIN film ON inventory.film_id = film.film_id
#         > WHERE film.rating = 'G'
#         > AND rental.rental_id IS NULL
#         > GROUP BY film.film_id;
```

By running this query, we obtain the same results from the database, but the `EXPLAIN` statement reveals a whole new execution plan in order to get the exact same results:

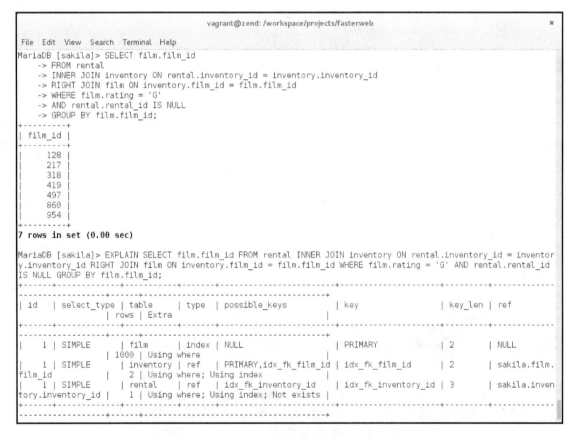

The new execution plan shows only 'SIMPLE' select types

The subqueries have disappeared and have become simple queries. Let's see what the performance schema recorded this time:

```
# MariaDB > SELECT EVENT_ID, TRUNCATE(TIMER_WAIT/1000000000000,6) as
Duration, SQL_TEXT
        > FROM performance_schema.events_statements_history_long WHERE
SQL_TEXT like '%GROUP BY%';
# MariaDB > SELECT event_name AS Stage,
TRUNCATE(TIMER_WAIT/1000000000000,6) AS Duration
        > FROM performance_schema.events_stages_history_long WHERE
NESTING_EVENT_ID=22717;
```

The profiler recorded the following results:

```
                            vagrant@zend: /workspace/projects/fasterweb                    ×

 File  Edit  View  Search  Terminal  Help
ventory.inventory_id RIGHT JOIN film ON inventory.film_id = film.film_id WHERE film.rating = 'G' AND rental.rent
al_id IS NULL GROUP BY film.film_id |
+----------+------+-----------------------------------------------------------------------------------------
-------------------------------------------------------------------------------------------------------------
-----------------------------------+
2 rows in set (0.00 sec)

MariaDB [performance_schema]> SELECT event_name AS Stage, TRUNCATE(TIMER_WAIT/1000000000000,6) AS Duration
    ->        FROM performance_schema.events_stages_history_long WHERE NESTING_EVENT_ID=22717;
+-------------------------------------+----------+
| Stage                               | Duration |
+-------------------------------------+----------+
| stage/sql/init                      | 0.000142 |
| stage/sql/checking permissions      | 0.000001 |
| stage/sql/checking permissions      | 0.000000 |
| stage/sql/checking permissions      | 0.000012 |
| stage/sql/Opening tables            | 0.000075 |
| stage/sql/After opening tables      | 0.000000 |
| stage/sql/System lock               | 0.000002 |
| stage/sql/Table lock                | 0.000000 |
| stage/sql/init                      | 0.000075 |
| stage/sql/optimizing                | 0.000034 |
| stage/sql/statistics                | 0.000035 |
| stage/sql/preparing                 | 0.000046 |
| stage/sql/Sorting result            | 0.000025 |
| stage/sql/executing                 | 0.000000 |
| stage/sql/Sending data              | 0.002636 |
| stage/sql/end                       | 0.000001 |
| stage/sql/query end                 | 0.000037 |
| stage/sql/closing tables            | 0.000000 |
| stage/sql/Unlocking tables          | 0.000031 |
| stage/sql/freeing items             | 0.000010 |
| stage/sql/cleaning up               | 0.000000 |
+-------------------------------------+----------+
21 rows in set (0.00 sec)

MariaDB [performance_schema]> █
```

The new query's profile reveals considerable performance improvements

The results clearly show that fewer optimization operations occurred in the initialization phases of the execution plan and that query execution as such was approximately seven times faster. Not all materialized subqueries can be optimized in this way but, when optimizing queries, a materialized subquery, a dependent subquery or an uncacheable subquery should always inspire us to ask ourselves if we can do any better.

For further information on query optimization, you can listen to a great presentation given on this topic by Michael Moussa at *Nomad PHP* (`https://nomadphp.com/product/mysql-analysis-understanding-optimization-queries/`).

Advanced benchmarking tools

Until now we have used the `mysqlslap` benchmarking tool. But, if you need to test your database server more thoroughly, other more advanced benchmarking tools do exist. We will have a quick look at two of these tools: DBT2 and SysBench.

DBT2

This benchmarking tool is used in order to run automated benchmarking tests against a MySQL server. It allows you to mimic large amounts of data warehouses.

To download, compile and install DBT2, please enter the following commands on the container's CLI:

```
# cd /srv/www
# wget -O dbt2-0.37.tar.gz
https://master.dl.sourceforge.net/project/osdldbt/dbt2/0.37/dbt2-0.37.tar.g
z
# tar -xvf dbt2-0.37.tar.gz
# cd dbt2-0.37.tar.gz
# ./configure --with-mysql
# make
# make install
# cpan install Statistics::Descriptive
# mkdir -p /srv/mysql/dbt2-tmp-data/dbt2-w3
# ./src/datagen -w 3 -d /srv/mysql/dbt2-tmp-data/dbt2-w3 --mysql
```

Once the data warehouses have been created, you should see the following messages:

```
vagrant@zend: /workspace/projects/fasterweb                          ✕

File  Edit  View  Search  Terminal  Help
root@1331adbe772a [ ~/dbt2-0.37 ]# ./src/datagen -w 3 -d /srv/mysql/dbt2-tmp-dat
a/dbt2-w3 --mysql
warehouses = 3
districts = 10
customers = 3000
items = 100000
orders = 3000
stock = 100000
new_orders = 900

Output directory of data files: /srv/mysql/dbt2-tmp-data/dbt2-w3

Generating data files for 3 warehouse(s)...
Generating item table data...
Finished item table data...
Generating warehouse table data...
Finished warehouse table data...
Generating stock table data...
Finished stock table data...
Generating district table data...
Finished district table data...
Generating customer table data...
Finished customer table data...
Generating history table data...
Finished history table data...
Generating order and order-line table data...
Finished order and order-line table data...
Generating new-order table data...
Finished new-order table data...
```

Confirmation that the database warehouses have been created

You will now have to modify the file `scripts/mysql/mysql_load_db.sh` using the vi editor:

```
# vi scripts/mysql/mysql_load_db.sh
```

Once inside the editor, type /LOAD DATA and press *Enter*. Position your cursor at the end of this line, press *I* and enter the word IGNORE in uppercase. Your file should look like this once you are done editing it:

```
                    vagrant@zend: /workspace/projects/fasterweb          ✕

 File  Edit  View  Search  Terminal  Help
for TABLE in $TABLES ; do

  echo "Loading table $TABLE"

  if [ "$TABLE" == "orders" ]; then
    FN="order"
  else
    FN="$TABLE"
  fi

  command_exec $MYSQL $DB_NAME -e \"LOAD DATA $LOCAL INFILE \\\"$DB_PATH/$FN.da
ta\\" IGNORE INTO TABLE $TABLE FIELDS TERMINATED BY '\t'\""

done

}


create_tables()
{

if [ "$DB_SCHEME" == "OPTIMIZED" ]; then
                                                      67,94            12%
```

Inserting the string "IGNORE" on the "LOAD DATA" line of the 'mysql_load_db.sh' script

Once done, press the *Esc* key and then type :wq. This will save the changes and close the vi editor.

Now, enter the following command to load the test data into the database:

```
# ./scripts/mysql/mysql_load_db.sh -d dbt2 -f /srv/mysql/dbt2-tmp-
data/dbt2-w3 -s /run/mysqld/mysqld.sock -u root
```

Once the data has been loaded into the database, you should see the following messages:

```
                        vagrant@zend: /workspace/projects/fasterweb           ×

 File  Edit  View  Search  Terminal  Help

Loading of DBT2 dataset located in /srv/mysql/dbt2-tmp-data/dbt2-w3 to database
dbt2.

DB_ENGINE:        INNODB
DB_SCHEME:        OPTIMIZED
DB_HOST:          localhost
DB_USER:          root
DB_SOCKET:        /run/mysqld/mysqld.sock

Creating table STOCK
Creating table ITEM
Creating table ORDER_LINE
Creating table ORDERS
Creating table NEW_ORDER
Creating table HISTORY
Creating table CUSTOMER
Creating table DISTRICT
Creating table WAREHOUSE

Loading table customer
Loading table district
Loading table history
Loading table item
Loading table new_order
Loading table order_line
Loading table orders
Loading table stock
Loading table warehouse
```

Confirmation that the data is being loaded into the database

To launch the test, enter this command:

```
# ./scripts/run_mysql.sh -n dbt2 -o /run/mysqld/mysqld.sock -u root -w 3 -t
300 -c 20
```

Once you have entered the command, you will first see this message:

Confirmation that the tests have begun

You will also get the following messages:

Confirmation that the tests are running

After approximately five minutes, you will get the results of the benchmark tests:

```
                        Response Time (s)
 Transaction     %      Average :     90th %        Total        Rollbacks         %
-------------   -----   ----------------------   -----------   ----------------   -----
    Delivery    3.92     0.029 :     0.059            18                0        0.00
   New Order   44.44     0.016 :     0.024           204                2        0.98
Order Status    3.49     0.003 :     0.014            16                0        0.00
     Payment   41.18     0.011 :     0.013           189                0        0.00
 Stock Level    4.58     0.010 :     0.031            21                0        0.00

39.10 new-order transactions per minute (NOTPM)
5.2 minute duration
0 total unknown errors
6 second(s) ramping up

cp: cannot stat 'notpm.input': No such file or directory
/root/dbt2-0.37
Test completed.
```

Confirmation that the tests are completed

As we can see from the given results, we can have a good idea of our database server's performance in the context of large data warehouses. Additional tests could easily confirm the server's limits through edge-case testing. Let's run one such test using SysBench.

SysBench

SysBench is another very popular open source benchmark testing tool. This tool not only allows you to test open source RDBMSs, but also your hardware (CPU, I/O, and so on).

To download, compile and install SysBench, please enter the following commands inside the Linux for PHP Docker container:

```
# cd /srv/www
# wget -O sysbench-0.4.12.14.tar.gz
https://downloads.mysql.com/source/sysbench-0.4.12.14.tar.gz
# tar -xvf sysbench-0.4.12.14.tar.gz
# cd sysbench-0.4.12.14
# ./configure
# make
# make install
```

Now, enter the following command to create a table with 1 million rows as the test data into the database:

```
# sysbench --test=oltp --oltp-table-size=1000000 --mysql-db=test --mysql-
user=root prepare
```

Once the data has been loaded into the database, you should see the following messages:

```
                    vagrant@zend: /workspace/projects/fasterweb              ×

  File  Edit  View  Search  Terminal  Help
root@ef9150c24e05 [ ~/sysbench-0.4.12.14 ]# sysbench --test=oltp --oltp-table-si
ze=1000000 --mysql-db=test --mysql-user=root prepare
sysbench 0.4.12.10:  multi-threaded system evaluation benchmark

No DB drivers specified, using mysql
Creating table 'sbtest'...
Creating 1000000 records in table 'sbtest'...
root@ef9150c24e05 [ ~/sysbench-0.4.12.14 ]# █
```

Confirmation that the test data has been loaded into the database

Now, to run the test, enter this command:

```
# sysbench --test=oltp --oltp-table-size=1000000 --mysql-db=test --mysql-
user=root --max-time=60 --oltp-read-only=on --max-requests=0 --num-
threads=8 run
```

Once you have entered the previous command, you will first get the following message:

```
                     vagrant@zend: /workspace/projects/fasterweb                    ×

 File  Edit  View  Search  Terminal  Help
root@ef9150c24e05 [ ~/sysbench-0.4.12.14 ]# sysbench --test=oltp --oltp-table-si
ze=1000000 --mysql-db=test --mysql-user=root --max-time=60 --oltp-read-only=on -
-max-requests=0 --num-threads=8 run
sysbench 0.4.12.10:  multi-threaded system evaluation benchmark

No DB drivers specified, using mysql
Running the test with following options:
Number of threads: 8
Random number generator seed is 0 and will be ignored


Doing OLTP test.
Running mixed OLTP test
Doing read-only test
Using Special distribution (12 iterations,  1 pct of values are returned in 75 p
ct cases)
Using "BEGIN" for starting transactions
Using auto_inc on the id column
Using 1 test tables
Threads started!
```

Confirmation that the tests are running

After a few minutes, you should get results similar to these:

```
                          vagrant@zend: /workspace/projects/fasterweb                    ×

   File   Edit   View   Search   Terminal   Help
(last message repeated 7 times)
Done.

OLTP test statistics:
    queries performed:
        read:                          1982190
        write:                         0
        other:                         283170
        total:                         2265360
    transactions:                      141585 (2359.52 per sec.)
    deadlocks:                         0        (0.00 per sec.)
    read/write requests:               1982190 (33033.25 per sec.)
    other operations:                  283170 (4719.04 per sec.)

General statistics:
    total time:                        60.0059s
    total number of events:            141585
    total time taken by event execution: 479.4936
    response time:
        min:                                0.62ms
        avg:                                3.39ms
        max:                               89.53ms
        approx.   95 percentile:            7.54ms

Threads fairness:
    events (avg/stddev):           17698.1250/3951.50
    execution time (avg/stddev):   59.9367/0.02

root@ef9150c24e05 [ ~/sysbench-0.4.12.14 ]# █
```

The results of the SysBench tests

The results show that the MariaDB server on my computer can handle approximately 2,300 transactions per second and 33,000 read/write requests per second. These edge-case tests can give us a very good idea of the general performance level that we can expect from our hardware and our database server.

Summary

In this chapter, we have learned how to measure and optimize database performance through the use of simple measurement techniques such as query optimization. Also, we have seen how to use advanced database benchmarking tools such as DBT2 and SysBench.

In the next chapter, we will see how to use modern SQL techniques in order to optimize very complex SQL queries.

6

Querying a Modern SQL Database Efficiently

We will now learn how to query an SQL database efficiently using Modern SQL. In this chapter, we will define what Modern SQL is and how to use it. We will start by defining the concept of Modern SQL and understanding what makes it different from traditional SQL by describing many of its features. Thus, we will acquire knowledge of how to convert certain traditional SQL queries into modern ones and when it is best to do so. Moreover, by doing so, we will better understand how Modern SQL can help us optimize a server's performance in more than one way.

Therefore, we will cover the following points:

- Understanding what Modern SQL is and its features
- Learning how and when to use `WITH` and `WITH RECURSIVE`, `CASE`, `OVER AND PARTITION BY`, `OVER AND ORDER BY`, GROUPING SETS, JSON clauses and functions, `FILTER` and `LATERAL` queries.

Modern SQL

What is Modern SQL and how does it distinguish itself from traditional SQL? What are its main features? Let's start by defining the concept itself.

Definition

As Markus Winand states on his website `https://modern-sql.com`, Modern SQL can be defined as *"an internationally standardized, widely available and Turing complete data processing language supporting relational and non-relational data models."* This definition refers to a set of standards that were promoted by the ISO and ANSI organizations over the years and that added new features to the SQL programming language. Since SQL-92, many new versions of the SQL standard were adopted and these standards introduced many new features based on relational and non-relational models. Here is a short list of these features with the corresponding standard that confirmed their adoption into the SQL language:

- `WITH` and `WITH RECURSIVE` (SQL:1999)
- `CASE` (SQL:1999 and SQL:2003)
- `OVER AND PARTITION BY` (SQL:2003 and SQL:2011)
- `OVER AND ORDER BY` (SQL:2003 and SQL:2011)
- GROUPING SETS (SQL:2011)
- JSON clauses and functions (SQL:2016)
- `FILTER` (SQL:2003)
- `LATERAL` queries (SQL:1999)

This being said, it should be noted that most of these features were not implemented by most **relational database management systems** (**RDBMSs**) until fairly recently. Most RDBMSs were only offering to their users, a more traditional SQL language based solely on the relational model promoted by the aging SQL-92 standard. It has only been in the most recent years that many, if not most, of RDBMSs have started implementing Modern SQL features.

Moreover, let's give this word of warning: using these features will not immediately yield great performance hikes for your database server. So, what is the point of using these features in your code base? The point is to make your code base compatible with future database engine optimizations and to avoid most problems related to slow query execution.

But, before looking further into the new SQL features, we will install `phpMyAdmin` inside our Linux for PHP container in order to see the results of our queries in a user-friendly fashion. To do so, please enter the following commands on the container's CLI:

```
# rm /srv/www
# ln -s /srv/fasterweb/chapter_6 /srv/www
# cd /srv
# wget -O phpMyAdmin-4.7.7-all-languages.zip
https://files.phpmyadmin.net/phpMyAdmin/4.7.7/phpMyAdmin-4.7.7-all-language
```

```
s.zip
# unzip phpMyAdmin-4.7.7-all-languages.zip
# cp phpMyAdmin-4.7.7-all-languages/config.sample.inc.php phpMyAdmin-4.7.7-
all-languages/config.inc.php
# sed -i "s/AllowNoPassword'] = false/AllowNoPassword'] = true/"
phpMyAdmin-4.7.7-all-languages/config.inc.php
# cd fasterweb/chapter_6
# ln -s ../../phpMyAdmin-4.7.7-all-languages ./phpmyadmin
```

These commands should make it possible to access the database server from a web interface at `http://localhost:8181/phpmyadmin`. When visiting this address via your favorite browser, you should see the following screen:

Enter your username and password on phpMyAdmin's login page

Once `phpMyAdmin` is installed, you can log in to the database server with the **Username** `root` and an empty **Password**.

Now, let's have a look at each one of these new SQL features in more detail.

WITH and WITH RECURSIVE

The first feature is what is known as a **Common Table Expression (CTE)**. A CTE is a temporary result set which allows you to join the same data to itself multiple times. There are two types of CTEs: non-recursive (`WITH`) and recursive (`WITH RECURSIVE`).

The non-recursive kind of CTE works like a derived table, allowing you to `SELECT` from a temporary result set. A simple example, using a fictitious staff table, would be:

```
WITH accountants AS (
  SELECT id, first_name, last_name
  FROM staff
  WHERE dept = 'accounting'
)
SELECT id, first_name, last_name
FROM accountants;
```

The recursive kind of CTE is composed of two parts. The first part of the query is what is called the anchor member of the CTE. The anchor's result set is what is considered to be the base result set (T_0). The second part is the recursive member which will run with T_i as input and T_{i+1} as output until an empty result set is returned. The query's final result set will be a `UNION ALL` between the recursive result set (T_n) and the anchor (T_0).

In order to better understand recursive CTEs and how useful they can be, let's give an example. But, before we begin, let's start by loading the following table into the test database. On the container's CLI, enter this command:

```
# mysql -uroot test < /srv/www/employees.sql
```

Once done, you can make sure that everything was loaded correctly by opening the database with `phpMyAdmin`, as seen here:

All the rows found in the employees table of the test database

In order to better understand CTEs, we will begin by using a basic query with multiple joins to obtain a hierarchical result set. To obtain the entire hierarchy of employees based solely on the presence of the manager's ID in the employee's record in the database, we would have to think of a query with multiple joins to the same table. In the SQL tab, enter this query:

```sql
SELECT CONCAT_WS('->', t1.last_name, t2.last_name, t3.last_name,
t4.last_name, t5.last_name, t6.last_name) AS path
FROM employees AS t1
RIGHT JOIN employees AS t2 ON t2.superior = t1.id
RIGHT JOIN employees AS t3 ON t3.superior = t2.id
RIGHT JOIN employees AS t4 ON t4.superior = t3.id
RIGHT JOIN employees AS t5 ON t5.superior = t4.id
RIGHT JOIN employees AS t6 ON t6.superior = t5.id
WHERE t1.superior IS NULL
ORDER BY path;
```

You will obtain this result set:

Hierarchical tree of all the employees generated with the JOIN statements

The first thing to notice is that this query presumes that we know in advance the number of levels in this hierarchy, which implies that we did a previous query to confirm this fact about our dataset. The second thing is the clumsiness of having to repeat the JOIN clauses in order to retrieve the entire result set. A recursive CTE is the perfect way to optimize such queries. To obtain the exact same result set with a recursive CTE, we would have to run the following query:

```
WITH RECURSIVE hierarchy_list AS (
  SELECT id, superior, CONVERT(last_name, CHAR(100)) AS path
  FROM employees
  WHERE superior IS NULL
  UNION ALL
  SELECT child.id, child.superior, CONVERT(CONCAT(parent.path, '->',
child.last_name), CHAR(100)) AS path
  FROM employees AS child
  INNER JOIN hierarchy_list AS parent ON (child.superior = parent.id)
)
SELECT path
```

```
FROM hierarchy_list
ORDER BY path;
```

If we were to compare the two previous queries by running them against MariaDB's performance schema, even though they do not offer the same functionality pertaining to the dynamic discovery of the number of levels in our hierarchy, we would get a better idea of what is going on under the hood.

Firstly, let's run the multiple join query with the EXPLAIN statement:

MariaDB's query execution plan with the JOIN statements

And now against the RDBMS's performance schema:

```
vagrant@zend: /workspace/projects/fasterweb                    ×

File  Edit  View  Search  Terminal  Help
| stage/sql/System lock           | 0.000005 |
| stage/sql/Table lock            | 0.000000 |
| stage/sql/init                  | 0.000034 |
| stage/sql/optimizing            | 0.000024 |
| stage/sql/statistics            | 0.000044 |
| stage/sql/preparing             | 0.000043 |
| stage/sql/Creating tmp table    | 0.000037 |
| stage/sql/Sorting result        | 0.000012 |
| stage/sql/executing             | 0.000000 |
| stage/sql/Sending data          | 0.000208 |
| stage/sql/Creating sort index   | 0.000030 |
| stage/sql/removing tmp table    | 0.000003 |
| stage/sql/end                   | 0.000002 |
| stage/sql/query end             | 0.000003 |
| stage/sql/closing tables        | 0.000001 |
| stage/sql/Unlocking tables      | 0.000006 |
| stage/sql/freeing items         | 0.000005 |
| stage/sql/cleaning up           | 0.000000 |
| stage/sql/init                  | 0.000024 |
| stage/sql/Opening tables        | 0.000022 |
| stage/sql/After opening tables  | 0.000000 |
| stage/sql/System lock           | 0.000000 |
| stage/sql/Table lock            | 0.000000 |
| stage/sql/init                  | 0.000004 |
| stage/sql/optimizing            | 0.000002 |
| stage/sql/statistics            | 0.000005 |
| stage/sql/preparing             | 0.000006 |
| stage/sql/executing             | 0.000000 |
| stage/sql/Filling schema table  | 0.000339 |
| stage/sql/executing             | 0.000000 |
| stage/sql/Sending data          | 0.000007 |
| stage/sql/end                   | 0.000000 |
| stage/sql/query end             | 0.000001 |
| stage/sql/closing tables        | 0.000000 |
| stage/sql/removing tmp table    | 0.000002 |
| stage/sql/Unlocking tables      | 0.000000 |
| stage/sql/freeing items         | 0.000001 |
| stage/sql/cleaning up           | 0.000000 |
+---------------------------------+----------+
65 rows in set (0.00 sec)
```

The multiple joins caused 65 operations in the database engine

Secondly, let's go through the same steps, but with the recursive CTE:

MariaDB's query execution plan with the recursive CTE

And, the performance schema should yield the following result:

```
                    vagrant@zend: /workspace/projects/fasterweb                    ×

 File  Edit  View  Search  Terminal  Help
 | stage/sql/optimizing          | 0.000004 |
 | stage/sql/optimizing          | 0.000004 |
 | stage/sql/statistics          | 0.000607 |
 | stage/sql/preparing           | 0.000016 |
 | stage/sql/optimizing          | 0.000008 |
 | stage/sql/statistics          | 0.000027 |
 | stage/sql/preparing           | 0.000013 |
 | stage/sql/statistics          | 0.000003 |
 | stage/sql/preparing           | 0.000002 |
 | stage/sql/Sorting result      | 0.000002 |
 | stage/sql/executing           | 0.000001 |
 | stage/sql/Sending data        | 0.000010 |
 | stage/sql/executing           | 0.000000 |
 | stage/sql/Sending data        | 0.000117 |
 | stage/sql/executing           | 0.000000 |
 | stage/sql/Sending data        | 0.000026 |
 | stage/sql/executing           | 0.000000 |
 | stage/sql/Sending data        | 0.000016 |
 | stage/sql/executing           | 0.000000 |
 | stage/sql/Sending data        | 0.000010 |
 | stage/sql/executing           | 0.000000 |
 | stage/sql/Sending data        | 0.000013 |
 | stage/sql/executing           | 0.000000 |
 | stage/sql/Sending data        | 0.000011 |
 | stage/sql/executing           | 0.000000 |
 | stage/sql/Sending data        | 0.000005 |
 | stage/sql/Creating sort index | 0.000104 |
 | stage/sql/end                 | 0.000003 |
 | stage/sql/removing tmp table  | 0.000002 |
 | stage/sql/removing tmp table  | 0.000000 |
 | stage/sql/query end           | 0.000003 |
 | stage/sql/closing tables      | 0.000000 |
 | stage/sql/removing tmp table  | 0.000001 |
 | stage/sql/removing tmp table  | 0.000000 |
 | stage/sql/Unlocking tables    | 0.000005 |
 | stage/sql/freeing items       | 0.000005 |
 | stage/sql/cleaning up         | 0.000000 |
 +-------------------------------+----------+
 47 rows in set (0.00 sec)

 MariaDB [test]> █
```

The CTE caused 47 operations in the database engine

Although this recursive CTE was a little slower than the basic multiple join query on my computer, it did generate fewer engine operations overall when all the selected columns were indexed. So, why is this more performant? A recursive CTE will allow you to avoid the hassle of creating a stored procedure, or something similar, in order to recursively discover the number of levels in your hierarchy tree, for example. This would most certainly make the multiple join query much slower if we added these operations to the main query. Also, a recursive CTE might be a kind of derived table that is not much quicker than a View and slightly slower than a basic multiple join query, but it is certainly very scalable and very useful when querying a database in order to walk a hierarchy tree, when using ranking functions or when modifying table contents based on a small result subset while resting assured that your more complex queries will benefit, for free, from future engine optimizations. Moreover, it will make your development cycle more efficient as it will make your code more readable to other developers by keeping it **DRY** ("**Don't Repeat Yourself**").

Let's move on to the next feature, the CASE expression.

CASE

Even though the CASE expression seems to remind us of imperative structures such as IF, SWITCH, and the like, it still does not allow for program flow control like those imperative structures, but rather allows for declarative evaluation of values based on certain conditions. Let's have a look at the following example in order to better understand this feature.

Please enter the following query in the SQL tab of the test database via the phpMyAdmin interface:

```
SELECT id, COUNT(*) as Total, COUNT(CASE WHEN superior IS NOT NULL THEN id
END) as 'Number of superiors'
FROM employees
WHERE id = 2;
```

This query should yield the following result set:

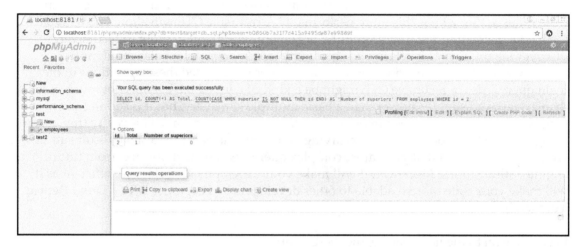

Result set of the query containing the CASE statement

As the result shows, the row with an id value of 2 was filtered out from the input of the second COUNT function as the CASE expression applied the condition which states that the superior column must not have a NULL value in order to count the id column. Using this feature of Modern SQL is not, for the most part, a question of added performance, but rather a question of avoiding stored procedures and controlling execution flows as much as possible, while keeping the code clean, easily readable and maintainable.

OVER and PARTITION BY

OVER and PARTITION BY are window functions that allow calculations to be done over a set of rows. Unlike aggregate functions, window functions do not group the results though. In order to better understand these two window functions, let's take the time to run the following query in the phpMyAdmin web interface:

```
SELECT DISTINCT superior AS manager_id, (SELECT last_name FROM employees
WHERE id = manager_id) AS last_name, SUM(salary) OVER(PARTITION BY
superior) AS 'payroll per manager'
FROM employees
WHERE superior IS NOT NULL
ORDER BY superior;
```

After running this query, you should see the following result:

List of managers with payroll per manager

As we can see, the result set shows the **payroll per manager** column without grouping the results. This is why we had to use the DISTINCT statement in order to avoid having multiple rows for the same manager. Obviously, window functions allow for efficient querying and optimized performance when doing aggregate calculations on subsets of rows that have some sort of relationship to the current row.

OVER AND ORDER BY

The OVER AND ORDER BY window functions are very useful when it comes to ranking within a subset of rows, calculating running totals or simply avoiding self-joins.

To illustrate when to use this most useful feature, we will take the previous example and determine the best paid employees on each payroll per manager by executing this query:

```
SELECT id, last_name, salary, superior AS manager_id, (SELECT last_name
FROM employees WHERE id = manager_id) AS manager_last_name, SUM(salary)
OVER(PARTITION BY superior ORDER BY manager_last_name, salary DESC, id) AS
payroll_per_manager
FROM employees
WHERE superior IS NOT NULL
ORDER BY manager_last_name, salary DESC, id;
```

Executing this query will give this result set:

List of the best paid employees on each payroll per manager

The returned result set allows us to see the breakdown of each payroll and ranks each employee within each subset. And what is the underlying execution plan that will allow us to get all these details about these subsets of data? The answer is a SIMPLE query! In the case of our query, there is a dependent subquery, but that is because we are fetching the last name of each manager in order to make the result set more interesting.

This would be the resulting query after removing the dependent subquery:

```
SELECT id, last_name, salary, superior AS manager_id, SUM(salary)
OVER(PARTITION BY superior ORDER BY manager_id, salary DESC, id) AS
payroll_per_manager
FROM employees
WHERE superior IS NOT NULL
ORDER BY manager_id, salary DESC, id;
```

And here is the underlying execution plan for this version of the same query:

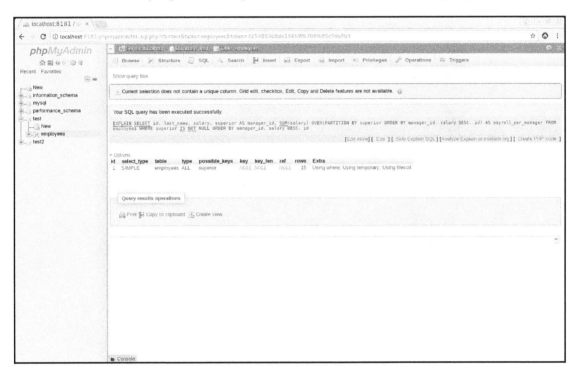

The query execution plan is simple when avoiding to fetch the last name of the manager

By running the query without the dependent subquery that was returning each manager's last name, the `select_type` of our query execution plan is `SIMPLE`. This makes for a highly efficient query that will be easily maintainable in the future.

GROUPING SETS

GROUPING SETS make it possible to apply many GROUP BY clauses in one single query. Moreover, this new feature introduces the notion of a ROLLUP, which is an extra row added to the result set that gives a summary of the results as a super-aggregate of previously returned values. Let's give a very simple example using the employees table in the test database. Let's execute the following query in the phpMyAdmin web interface:

```
SELECT superior AS manager_id, SUM(salary)
FROM employees
WHERE superior IS NOT NULL
GROUP BY manager_id, salary;
```

Once executed, you should see this result:

GROUPING SETS make it possible to apply many GROUP BY clauses in one single query

The multiple GROUP BY clauses have allowed us to quickly see each individual salary of each employee under the supervision of each manager. If we now add the ROLLUP operator to the GROUP BY clauses, we will obtain this result:

The result set when adding the ROLLUP operator to the GROUP BY clauses

The ROLLUP operator adds extra rows that contain a super-aggregate result for each subset and for the entire result set. The execution plan reveals that the underlying select_type is once more SIMPLE instead of having multiple queries united with a UNION operator as we would have done before this feature existed. Once more, Modern SQL offers us a highly optimized query which will remain highly maintainable for many years to come.

JSON clauses and functions

One of the latest additions to the SQL language is the JSON features. This new group of features makes it easier to benefit from the advantages of storing certain types of unstructured and schema-less data like the JSON format in a very structured and relational way using SQL native functions. This allows for many things, such as applying integrity contraints on certain JSON fields contained in a JSON document, indexing certain JSON fields, easily converting and returning unstructured data into relational data and vice versa, and inserting or updating unstructured data by the means of the proven reliability of SQL transactions.

To fully appreciate this new group of features, let's insert some data into the test database by executing a query that will convert the JSON data into relational data.

First, please execute the following command on the container's CLI:

```
# mysql -uroot test < /srv/www/json_example.sql
```

Once the new table is loaded into the database, you can execute the following query:

```
SELECT id,
    JSON_VALUE(json,  "$.name")  AS name,
    JSON_VALUE(json,  "$.roles[0]")  AS main_role,
    JSON_VALUE(json,  "$.active")  AS active
FROM json_example
WHERE id = 1;
```

Once executed, you should see this result:

The JSON functions automatically convert the JSON data into relational data

As we can see, converting JSON unstructured data into relational and structured data was very easy using the new JSON functions. Inserting unstructured data into a structured database is just as easy. Moreover, the added constraint would verify that the JSON string being inserted is valid. To verify this feature, let's attempt to insert invalid JSON data into our test table:

```
INSERT INTO `json_example` (`id`, `json`) VALUES (NULL, 'test');
```

Upon trying to execute the query, we would get the following error message:

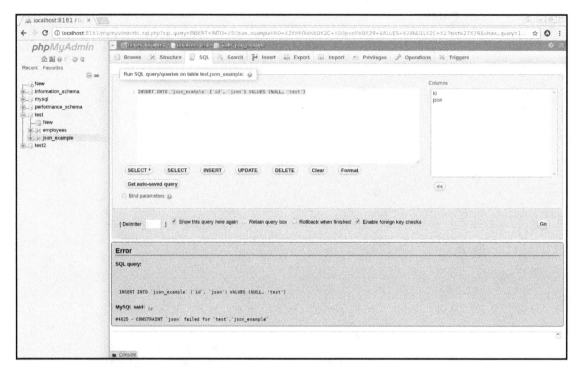

The JSON constraints make sure that the JSON string being inserted is valid

Thus, Modern SQL makes working with JSON-formatted data easy in an SQL environment. This will greatly optimize performance at the application level, as it will now be possible to eliminate the overhead that comes with having to `json_encode()` and `json_decode()` every time an application needs to retrieve or store JSON-formatted data into a relational database.

There are many more Modern SQL features that we could try to better understand, but not all RDBMSs have implemented them and many of these features would require that we analyze implementation details. We will simply look at two more features that have not been implemented within the MariaDB server, but that have been within the PostgreSQL server. In order to start and use the PostgreSQL server that is included in the Linux for PHP container, please enter the following commands on the container's CLI:

```
# /etc/init.d/postgresql start
# cd /srv
# wget --no-check-certificate -O phpPgAdmin-5.1.tar.gz
```

```
https://superb-sea2.dl.sourceforge.net/project/phppgadmin/phpPgAdmin%20%5Bs
table%5D/phpPgAdmin-5.1/phpPgAdmin-5.1.tar.gz
# tar -xvf phpPgAdmin-5.1.tar.gz
# sed -i "s/extra_login_security'] = true/extra_login_security'] = false/"
phpPgAdmin-5.1/conf/config.inc.php
# cd fasterweb/chapter_6
# ln -s ../../phpPgAdmin-5.1 ./phppgadmin
# cd /srv/www
```

After entering these commands, you should be able to access the PostgreSQL server via the `phpPgAdmin` web interface at `http://localhost:8181/phppgadmin`. Point your browser to this address and click on the **Servers** icon in the upper right-hand corner of the screen in order to see the following interface:

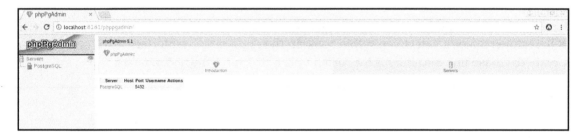

Only one available PostgreSQL server is listed and is accessible through port 5432

From here, click on the **PostgreSQL** link in the center of the page, type `postgres` as the **Username** and leave the **Password** empty on the login page:

On the login page, type in the username 'postgres' and the leave the password box empty

Then, click on the **Login** button and you should be able to access the server:

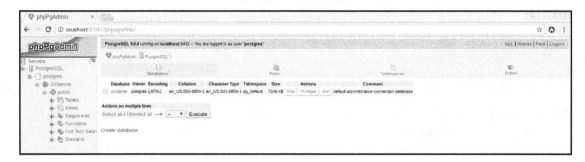

The server displays **postgres** as its only available database

Finally, we will create a database that will allow us to learn how to use the two last Modern SQL features that we will cover in this book. In the `phpPgAdmin` interface, click on the **Create database** link and fill out the form in order to create the test database:

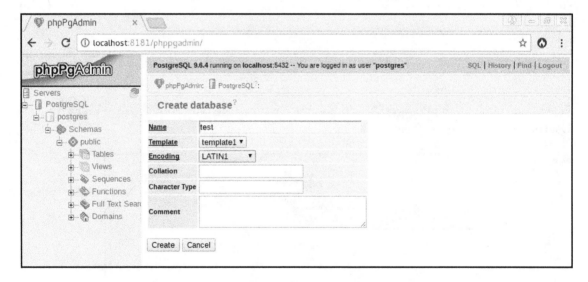

Create the database test with the template1 template and an encoding of LATIN1

By clicking on the **Create** button, you will create the test database alongside the postgres database:

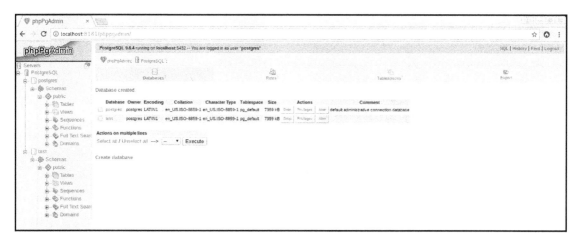

Now, the server displays the test database alongside the postgres database

Once this is done, enter the following commands on the container's CLI:

```
# su postgres
# psql test < sales.sql
# exit
```

We are now ready to try out the FILTER clause.

FILTER

Another very interesting feature of Modern SQL is the FILTER clause. It makes it possible to add WHERE clauses to aggregation functions. Let's try the FILTER clause by executing the following query in the SQL tab of the test database in the phpPgAdmin interface:

```
SELECT
    SUM(total) as total,
    SUM(total) FILTER(WHERE closed IS TRUE) as transaction_complete,
    year
FROM sales
GROUP BY year;
```

You should get the following result:

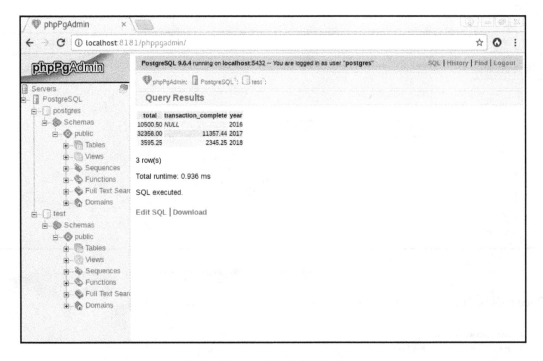

Result set of the query containing the FILTER statement

The FILTER clause is great for generating reports without adding too much overhead in the query's WHERE clauses.

Moreover, a FILTER clause is great for pivot tables, where grouping by year and month is made more complicated by the fact that it is necessary to generate a report that must cross month and year on two different axes (month = x and year = y, for example).

Let's continue with the last Modern SQL feature, LATERAL queries.

LATERAL queries

LATERAL queries allow you to select more than one column and one row in a correlated subquery. This is very useful when creating Top-N subqueries and trying to join table functions together, thus making unnesting them a clear possibility. The LATERAL query can then be thought of as a sort of SQL foreach loop.

Let's give a simple example that would illustrate how a LATERAL query would work. Let's say that we have two hypothetical tables that contain data on films and actors:

```
SELECT
     film.id,
     film.title,
     actor_bio.name,
     actor_bio.biography
FROM film,
     LATERAL (SELECT
                  actor.name,
                  actor.biography
              FROM actor
              WHERE actor.film_id = film.id) AS actor_bio;
```

As we can see, the LATERAL subquery is selecting multiple columns from the actor table (actor.name and actor.biography) while still being able to correlate references from the film table (film.id). Many optimizations, whether it be performance optimizations or code readability and maintainability, become a real possibility with LATERAL queries.

For further information on Modern SQL, I invite you to consult *Markus Winand*'s excellent website (https://modern-sql.com), and listen to *Elizabeth Smith*'s great presentation on this topic at *Nomad PHP* (https://nomadphp.com/product/modern-sql/).

Summary

In this chapter, we have learned how to query an SQL database efficiently using Modern SQL. We have defined what Modern SQL is and how we can use it. We have acquired knowledge of how to convert certain traditional SQL queries into modern ones and when it is best to do so. Moreover, by doing so, we now better understand how Modern SQL can help us optimize a server's performance in more than one way.

In the next chapter, we will cover a few of JavaScript's best and worst parts, especially those that pertain to code efficiency and overall performance, and how a developer should always write safe, reliable and highly efficient JavaScript code, mostly by avoiding *danger-driven development*.

7
JavaScript and Danger-Driven Development

"In JavaScript, there is a beautiful, elegant, highly expressive language that is buried under a steaming pile of good intentions and blunders."

— Douglas Crockford, JavaScript: The Good Parts

This quotation expresses essentially what optimizing JavaScript code is all about.

Often fascinated by the latest shiny feature or by the need to deliberately or pretentiously display his own abilities, the developer's mind sometimes slips into a mysterious state of awaken sleep by which he is overcome by the need to show off overly complex code or by the desire to use the most recent features even though he knows, deep down, that this means that he will have to sacrifice long-term stability and the efficiency of his computer program. This way of building applications is what we might call "Danger-Driven Development". JavaScript has many very bad parts but has enough good parts to outweigh the bad ones. This being said, the problem with Danger-Driven Development is the fact that the developer listens to the sirens of JavaScript's awful parts at the expense of the end user's satisfaction.

In this chapter, we will cover a few of JavaScript's best and worst parts, especially those that pertain to code efficiency and overall performance, and how a developer should always write safe, reliable and highly efficient JavaScript code even if doing so is not as enchanting as coding the latest shiny.

Thus, we will cover the following points:

- The global object and local variables
- Avoiding bad idioms and keeping an eye on the very bad parts
- Using the DOM efficiently
- Structuring and loading a JavaScript application

The global object and local variables

JavaScript's global object is the container of all global variables. Any top-level variable of any compilation unit will be stored in the global object. The global object is one of the worst parts of JavaScript when it is not used correctly, as it can easily become bloated with unneeded variables and can be unknowingly abused by developers when JavaScript default behavior is heavily relied upon. Here are two examples of such misuse:

- When running a simple code such as `total = add(3, 4);`, you are, in fact, creating a property named `total` in the global object. This is not a good thing for performance as you might keep a lot of variables on the heap while most of them are only required at a certain moment of an application's execution.
- When neglecting to use the `new` keyword in order to create an object, JavaScript will execute an ordinary function call and will bind the `this` variable to the global object. This is a very bad thing, not only for security reasons, as it is possible to clobber other variables, but also for performance reasons as the developer might think that he is storing values in an object's properties while he is, in fact, storing these values in the global object directly, thus bloating the global object and storing these values in two different memory spaces if he already instantiated the desired object elsewhere in his code.

To use the global object efficiently, you should wrap all your variables in a single application object, apply functions to it as needed, enforce type verification within the functions that you are applying to the application object in order to make sure that it is instantiated correctly and access the global object by thinking of it as a sort of immutable object with a few side-effect functions that are the application objects.

Avoiding global variables

Global variables can be accessed for reading or writing in any scope of an application. They are a necessary evil. Indeed, any application needs to organize its code structure in order to process input values and return the appropriate response or output. Problems and bugs start occurring when the code is not well organized and when any part of the code can therefore modify the global state of the rest of the application and modify the program's overall expected behavior.

Firstly, poorly organized code means that the scripting engine, or interpreter, has more work to do when trying to look up a variable name, because it will have to go through many scopes until it finds it in the global scope.

Secondly, poorly organized code means that the heap in memory will always be larger than needed to run the same functionality, since many superfluous variables will remain in memory until the end of the script's execution.

The solution to this problem is to avoid using global variables as much as possible and to use namespaced variables almost all the time. Also, using locally scoped variables has the added advantage of making sure that variables are automatically unset when the local scope is lost.

The following example (`chap7_js_variables_1.html`) shows us how the use of global variables can be very problematic and ultimately very inefficient, especially in increasing complex applications:

```
<!DOCTYPE html>

<html lang="en">
<head>
    <meta charset="UTF-8">
    <title>JS Variables</title>

    <meta name="viewport" content="width=device-width, initial-scale=1">
</head>

<body onload="myJS()" style="margin:0;">

<div id="main"></div>

<script type="text/javascript">

    function Sum(n1, n2)
    {
        // These will be global when called from the myJSAgain() function.
```

```
        this.number1 = Number(n1);
        this.number2 = Number(n2);

        return this.number1 + this.number2;
    }

    function myJS()
    {
        // Side-effect: creates a global variable named 'total'.
        total = new Sum(3, 4);
        alert( window.total ); // Object

        // Side-effect: modifies the global variable named 'total'.
        myJSAgain();

        // Global 'total' variable got clobbered.
        alert( window.total ); // 3
    }

    function myJSAgain()
    {
        // Missing 'new' keyword. Will clobber the global 'total' variable.
        total = Sum(1, 2);

        // There are now two sets of 'number1' and 'number2' variables!
        alert( window.number2 ); // 2
    }

</script>

</body>

</html>
```

The easy solution is to organize the code by using modules and namespaces. This is easily achieved by wrapping all variables and functions within a single application object in order to force a certain associated behavior when the variables are set or modified, and to preserve the application's secrets from the global object. Closures can also be used to hide important values from the global scope. Let's modify our previous script, keeping namespaces in mind this time:

```
function myJS()
    {
        function MyJSObject(n1, n2)
        {
            var number1 = Number(n1);
            var number2 = Number(n2);
```

```
        return {
            set_number1: function (n1) {
                number1 = Number(n1);
            },
            set_number2: function (n2) {
                number2 = Number(n2);
            },
            sum: function ( ) {
                return number1 + number2;
            }
        };
    }

    var oApp1 = new MyJSObject(3, 4);
    alert( oApp1.sum() ); // 7

    var app2 = MyJSObject(1, 2);
    alert( app2.sum() ); // 3
    alert( oApp1.sum() ); // 7
    alert( window.number1 ); // undefined
}
```

By using the `let` keyword in this way, the developer would still obtain the correct value while avoiding to clobber a global variable and unintentionally modifying the global state of the entire application, even if he was to forget to use the `new` keyword. Furthermore, the global object remains lean and efficient by avoiding unnecessary bloat and by reducing time spent in namespace lookups in order to find a called function or a stored value.

Evaluating local variables

As we have seen in the previous example, omitting the `let` or `var` keyword in front of the declaration of a local variable makes it global. In all cases, functions and objects should not be able to create functional side effects by modifying the value of variables outside of their local scope. Thus, the `let` keyword should always be used when declaring variables inside the scope of a function or structure. For example, simply moving global variables to the local scope of a function that is using them within a local loop translates into almost a 30% increase in performance in most browsers.

Also, when declaring variables with the `let` keyword, you get to use block scope, which should be used as much as possible. Thus, a variable used within a `for` loop will not stay within scope once the loop is done. This allows for better variable encapsulation and isolation, more efficient garbage collection and better performance in general.

One way to easily keep track of variable declarations is to use JavaScript's strict mode. We will explain this ES5 feature in more detail in the next section of this chapter.

Avoiding bad idioms and keeping an eye on the very bad parts

As with most C-based programming languages, it is best to avoid certain bad idioms that often cause code inefficiency and bugs.

Bad idioms

Here are a few bad idioms that should be identified as problematic:

- Declaring a variable at first use is a bad idea in JavaScript due to the fact that the developer will most likely give the variable global scope in order to access it later. It is better to organize the code from the start of the project and use intuitive and meaningful namespaces in order to organize the use of variables throughout the application.
- Using structures in a way that is not explicit or that was not originally intended should be avoided in all cases. For example, letting a `switch` statement fall through or assigning a value to a variable within the condition of a conditional statement are very bad idioms and should never be used.
- Relying on automatic semicolon insertion is a bad idea and can lead to code misinterpretation. It should always be avoided.
- Trailing commas in arrays and objects is a bad idea since some browsers will not interpret them correctly.
- When using a `block` statement with one single imperative line, omitting the curly braces should be avoided at all times.

Of course, the art of structuring code adequately relies foremost upon a good knowledge of the structures themselves. There are bad constructs in JavaScript that should be avoided at all times. Let's take the time to look at a few.

Bad constructs – the with statement

One example of these bad constructs is the `with` statement. The original intention of the `with` statement was to help developers access object properties without having to type the whole namespace every time. It was intended to be a sort of `use` statement as we might encounter them in other languages like PHP. For example, you could use the `with` statement in the following way:

```
foo.bar.baz.myVar    = false;
foo.bar.baz.otherVar = false;

with (foo.bar.baz) {
    myVar = true;
    otherVar = true;
}
```

The problem here is that, when we are looking at this code, we are not entirely sure that the engine is not clobbering global variables named `myVar` and `otherVar`. The best way to deal with long namespaces is to assign them to local variables and use them afterwards:

```
let fBrBz = foo.bar.baz;

fBrBz.myVar = true;
fBrBz.otherVar = true;
```

Bad constructs – the eval statement

Another bad one is the `eval()` statement. This statement is not only very inefficient, but it is, most of the time, useless. Indeed, it is often believed that using the `eval()` statement is the proper way to deal with a provided string. But this is not the case. You can simply use an array syntax to do the same thing. For example, we could use the `eval()` statement in the following way:

```
function getObjectProperty(oString)
{
    let oRef;
    eval("oRef = foo.bar.baz." + oString);
    return oRef;
}
```

To get a substantial speed increase (from 80% to 95% faster), you could replace the previous code with the following:

```
function getObjectProperty(oString)
{
    return foo.bar.baz[oString];
}
```

Bad constructs – the try-catch-finally construct

It is important to note that one should avoid using the try-catch-finally construct inside performance-critical functions. The reason is related to the fact that this construct must create a runtime variable to catch the exception object. This runtime creation is a special case in JavaScript and not all browsers handle it with the same degree of efficiency, which means that this operation can cause trouble along the application's critical path, especially when performance is crucial. You can easily replace this construct with simple testing conditions and insert error messages in an object that would act as error registry for the application.

Avoiding inefficient loops

Nesting loops is the first thing to avoid when coding these types of structures in JavaScript.

Also, most of the time, using `for-in` loops is not a good idea since the engine has to create a complete list of the enumerable properties, which is not very efficient. Most times, a `for` loop will do the job perfectly. This is particularly true of performance-critical functions that are found along the critical path of the application.

Furthermore, beware of implicit object conversions when dealing with loops. Often, at first glance, it is difficult to see what is happening under the hood when repeatedly accessing a `length` property on an object for example. But there are cases where JavaScript will create an object on each iteration of a loop when the object is not specifically created beforehand. Please see the following code example (`chap7_js_loops_1.html`):

```
function myJS()
{
    let myString = "abcdefg";

    let result = "";

    for(let i = 0; i < myString.length; i++) {
```

```
        result += i + " = " + myString.charAt(i) + ", ";
        console.log(myString);
    }

    alert(result);
}
```

When having a look at the console results in Google Chrome's **Developer tools**, we get the following result:

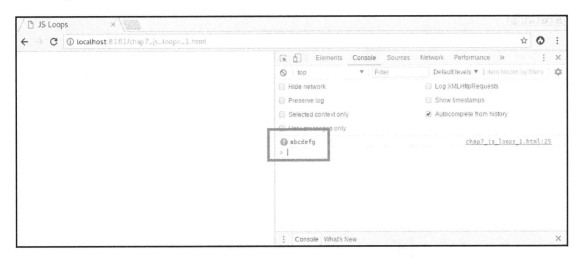

Seven string objects were created in all, one on each iteration of the 'for' loop

Under the hood, the JavaScript engine is actually creating a string object on each iteration of the loop. In order to avoid this problem, we will explicitly instantiate a string object before entering the loop (`chap7_js_loops_2.html`):

```
function myJS()
{
    let oMyString = new String("abcdefg");

    let result = "";

    for(let i = 0; i < oMyString.length; i++) {
        result += i + " = " + oMyString.charAt(i) + ", ";
        console.log(oMyString);
    }

    alert(result);
}
```

The results of the new script are as shown:

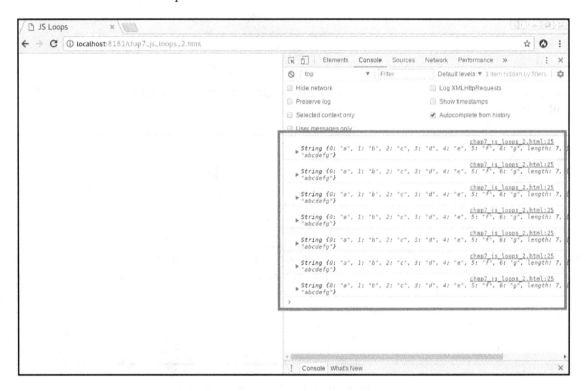

Only one object is created and is shown seven times

The console's log is now showing us the same object seven times. It is easy to understand how this could optimize the performance of a loop, especially when the loop could cause the engine to create tens, hundreds or even thousands of objects in order to complete its work.

Linters and strict mode

There are some other bad parts in JavaScript that could cause performance issues on some occasions. In order to keep an eye on all of these bad parts and replace them with JavaScript's good parts, it is highly recommended that you use a tool that will allow you to find issues with a piece of code even before you run it for the first time. These tools are linters.

JSLint, ESLint, and *Prettier* are tools that can help you find sloppy code and fix it, even automatically in some cases. Some linters, such as *ESLint,* might even help you improve your code by reducing the number of statements, reducing the nesting of structures by replacing them with functions and Promises, identifying cyclomatic complexity—which is measuring the number of branches a single piece of structural code has—and maybe allowing you to replace those structural pieces of code with more functional ones, as we will see in the next chapter. You can find these tools at the following addresses:

- `http://www.jslint.com/`
- `https://eslint.org/`
- `https://github.com/prettier/prettier`

An added benefit of using linters is the fact that they make JavaScript code compatible with ES5's strict mode. Whenever possible, strict mode should be used. It is as easy as adding a `use strict;` statement at the beginning of a script or a function in order to use it. Amongst the many benefits of using strict mode is a simplified mapping of variable names to variable definitions (optimized namespace lookups), prohibition of the `with` statement, prevention of unexpected introduction of variables into the current scope through the use of `eval` statements, protection against "boxing" (forced instantiation) of the `this` variable when it is not containing an object and it is passed to a function, which reduces performance cost considerably, and the removal of most performance preclusions, such as accessing the function caller's variables and "walking" the JavaScript stack at runtime.

Many excellent books and videos on JavaScript performance have been published by Packt Publishing and I highly recommend that you read them in order to master all these fine tools.

Using the DOM efficiently

Document Object Model (DOM) manipulations remain amongst the costliest operations to do in JavaScript. Indeed, repaints or reflows should be kept to a bare minimum in order to avoid performance issues in general.

This being said though, there are other pitfalls that must be avoided in order to maintain the speed of a script when DOM operations are required and lead to repaints or reflows. These pitfalls concern how to modify the document tree, how to update an invisible element, how to make style changes, how to search for nodes, how to manage references from one document to another and what to do when inspecting a large number of nodes.

Modifying the document tree

It is important to know that making modifications while traversing the tree is very expensive. It is best to create a temporary collection to work on rather than modifying the tree directly while looping over all of its nodes.

Indeed, the best approach is to use a non-displayed DOM tree fragment, to make all the changes at once and then, to display them all together. Here is a theoretical example of how this can be accomplished:

```
function myJS()
{
    let docFragment = document.createDocumentFragment();
    let element, content;
    for(let i = 0; i < list.length; i++) {
        element = document.createElement("p");
        content = document.createTextNode(list[i]);
        element.appendChild(content);
        docFragment.appendChild(element);
    }
    document.body.appendChild(docFragment);
}
```

It is also possible to clone an element in order to modify it completely before triggering a reflow of the page. The following code shows how this can be done:

```
function myJS()
{
    let container = document.getElementById("container1");
    let cloned = container.cloneNode(true);
    cloned.setAttribute("width", "50%");
    let element, content;
    for(let i = 0; i < list.length; i++) {
        element = document.createElement("p");
        content = document.createTextNode(list[i]);
        element.appendChild(content);
        cloned.appendChild(element);
    }
    container.parentNode.replaceChild(cloned, container);
}
```

By using these techniques, a developer would avoid some of the costliest operations in JavaScript in terms of performance.

Updating an invisible element

Another technique is to set an element's display style to none. Thus, it will not need a repaint when its content is being changed. Here is a code example that shows how this can be done:

```
function myJS()
{
    let container = document.getElementById("container1");

    container.style.display = "none";
    container.style.color = "red";
    container.appendChild(moreNodes);
    container.style.display = "block";
}
```

This is an easy and quick way to modify a node while avoiding multiple repaints or reflows.

Making style changes

In the same way as when we mentioned how to modify many nodes at once when traversing the DOM tree, it is possible to make many style changes simultaneously on a document fragment in order to minimize the number of repaints or reflows. Take the following code snippet as an example:

```
function myJS()
{
    let container = document.getElementById("container1");
    let modifStyle = "background: " + newBackgound + ";" +
        "color: " + newColor + ";" +
        "border: " + newBorder + ";";
    if(typeof(container.style.cssText) != "undefined") {
        container.style.cssText = modifStyle;
    } else {
        container.setAttribute("style", modifStyle);
    }
}
```

As we can see, any number of style attributes could be modified in this way in order to trigger only one repaint or reflow.

Searching for nodes

When searching for nodes through the entire DOM, it best to use XPath to do so. Often, a `for` loop is used, as per the following example where h2, h3 and h4 elements are being searched for:

```
function myJS()
{
    let elements = document.getElementsByTagName("*");
    for(let i = 0; i < elements.length; i++) {
        if(elements[i].tagName.match("/^h[2-4]$/i")) {
            // Do something with the node that was found
        }
    }
}
```

Instead of using this `for` loop, an XPath iterator object could be used to obtain the same result, only much more efficiently:

```
function myJS()
{
    let allHeadings = document.evaluate("//h2|//h3|//h4", document, null,
XPathResult.ORDERED_NODE_ITERATOR_TYPE, null);
    let singleheading;
    while(singleheading = allHeadings.iterateNext()) {
        // Do something with the node that was found
    }
}
```

Using XPath with a DOM containing more than a thousand nodes will definitely make a difference performance-wise.

Inspecting a large number of nodes

Another pitfall to avoid is trying to inspect a large number of nodes at once. It is much better to narrow down the search to a specific subset of nodes and then use built-in methods to find the desired nodes. For example, if we know that the node we are looking for can be found inside a specific `div` element, then we could use the following code example:

```
function myJS()
{
    let subsetElements = document.getElementById("specific-
div").getElementsByTagName("*");
```

```
    for(let i = 0; i < subsetElements.length; i++) {
        if(subsetElements[i].hasAttribute("someattribute")) {
            // Do something with the node that was found...
            break;
        }
    }
}
```

Thus, this search will be much more efficient and return results much faster than if we had searched for it within a large number of nodes.

Managing references from one document to another

When managing references to many documents within JavaScript, it is important to destroy these references when a document is no longer needed. For example, if a document was in a pop-up window, in a frame, in an inline frame or in an object, and the document was dismissed by the user, the document's nodes will remain in memory and will continue to bloat the DOM. Destroying these unused references can improve performance considerably.

Caching DOM values

When accessing an object repeatedly, it is much more efficient to store it in a local variable in order to use it over and over again. For example, the following code makes a local copy of the grouped DOM values instead of accessing each value separately:

```
function myJS()
{
    let group = document.getElementById("grouped");

    group.property1 = "value1";
    group.property2 = "value2";
    group.property3 = "value3";
    group.property4 = "value4";
    // Instead of:
    //
    // document.getElementById("grouped").property1 = "value1";
    // document.getElementById("grouped").property2 = "value2";
    // document.getElementById("grouped").property3 = "value3";
    // document.getElementById("grouped").property4 = "value4";
}
```

Doing so will allow you to avoid the performance overhead associated with dynamic lookups.

Structuring and loading a JavaScript application

When thinking of how to structure and load a JavaScript application, it is important to remember certain important principles.

Minimizing costly operations

The costliest operations to do in JavaScript are:

- Requesting a resource through network I/O
- Display repainting, also known as redrawing, of the web page due to dynamic content changes such as making an element visible
- Reflowing, which can be caused by a window resize
- A DOM manipulation or dynamic change to the page's styling

Obviously, the bottom line is that all these operations should be kept to a bare minimum in order to preserve good performance in general. When working on a script that is executing too slowly, these are the most important elements to look for with Google Chrome's Timeline tool, which can be accessed through Chrome's Developer tools, as mentioned in Chapter 1, *Faster Web – Getting Started*, of this book.

Cleaning up, minifying, and compressing resources

Of course, excluding unused exports from bundles, also known as tree shaking, minifying scripts by cleaning up dead code and then, compressing script files, is always a good thing when it comes to JavaScript performance, especially when dealing with network latency. Amongst the very good tools that will help you do this is *Webpack* (https://webpack.js. org/), combined with the *UglifyJS* plugin (https://github.com/webpack-contrib/ uglifyjs-webpack-plugin) and its compression plugin (https://github.com/webpack-contrib/compression-webpack-plugin), which will tree-shake your code, minify your script by removing any unused or dead code, and compress the resulting files.

The advantages of tree-shaking will be felt mostly when using tree shaking third-party dependencies. In order to better understand how to use these tools, it is highly recommended that you have a look at the following tutorials:

- `http://2ality.com/2015/12/webpack-tree-shaking.html`
- `https://medium.com/@roman01la/dead-code-elimination-and-tree-shaking-in-javascript-build-systems-fb8512c86edf`

Another great tool to optimize JavaScript code (tree-shake, minify, and compress) is Google's *Closure*, even though it is built with Java. You will find this tool at the following address: `https://developers.google.com/closure/`.

Loading page resources

It is important to avoid blocking a page's rendering when loading the script files in the head section of the HTML document. Scripts should always be loaded at the end of the body section in order to make sure that rendering will not depend on network latency that might occur when fetching the required JavaScript files.

Also, it is important to know that it is best to place inline scripts before CSS stylesheets, as CSS will often prevent the scripts from running until they have finished downloading.

Also, splitting the script file payloads and downloading scripts asynchronously are all techniques that must be thought out when structuring a JavaScript application for performance.

Furthermore, *Steve Souders* has written many great books and articles on boosting web page performance and you should read them to get more information on these very important techniques and principles (`https://stevesouders.com/`).

Caching page resources

Another important thing to remember, as we will see in more detail in `Chapter 9`, *Boosting a Web Server's Performance*, is that caching techniques, both on the server side and on the client side, will help you significantly boost the performance of your web pages. Leveraging these techniques will allow you to reduce the number of requests needed to simply get the same JavaScript files over and over again.

Summary

In this chapter, we have covered a few of JavaScript's best and worst parts, especially the pitfalls that can cause issues performance-wise. We have seen how coding safe, reliable and highly-efficient JavaScript code might not be as exciting as using the latest shiny feature or as tempting as lazy coding, but will certainly help any JavaScript application be a part of the Faster Web.

In the next chapter, we will see how JavaScript is increasingly becoming a functional language and how this programming paradigm will be a vector for performance in the near future. We will take a quick look at upcoming language features that will help improve the performance of JavaScript applications.

8
Functional JavaScript

The future of JavaScript will be functional. Indeed, many changes that were brought to the language in the last few years are allowing for easier and more efficient implementations when using functional programming techniques.

In this chapter, we will see how JavaScript is increasingly becoming a functional language and how this programming paradigm can be a vector for performance. We will learn how replacing overly complex code with simplified functional versions and how using immutability and tail-call optimization will help make JavaScript more efficient in the long run. Thus, we will cover the following points:

- Simplifying functions
- Functional programming techniques
- More upcoming JavaScript features

Simplifying functions

Traditionally, computer science students are told to keep their functions simple. It is often said that one function should correspond to one single action. Indeed, the more a function has cyclomatic complexity, the harder it is to reuse, maintain and test. The more a function becomes a purely logical being that has no real-world roots in a clearly identifiable action, the harder it is to grasp and use in combination with other functions.

Functional programming principles

The **functional programming** (**FP**) paradigm pushes this reasoning further by considering computational design as being based on mathematical functions and the immutability of state and data. FP's guiding principle is that the entire computer program should be a single, referentially transparent expression. At its core, the concept of FP requires that functions be pure, referentially transparent and free of side effects. A function is pure when, given the same input, it always returns the same output. It is referentially transparent when its functional expression is interchangeable with its corresponding value anywhere inside a computer program. It is free of side effects when it does not modify an application's state outside of its scope. Thus, for example, modifying a variable that is declared outside of its scope or echoing a message to a screen are considered to be functional side effects that must be avoided as much as possible.

An example of a pure function would be as follows:

```
function myJS()
{
    function add(n1, n2)
    {
        let number1 = Number(n1);
        let number2 = Number(n2);

        return number1 + number2;
    }

}
```

The next function is not pure, because there are two side effects:

```
function myJS()
{
    function add(n1, n2)
    {
        // 1. Modifies the global scope
        let number1 = Number(n1);
        let number2 = Number(n2);

        // 2. The alert function
        alert( number1 + number2 );
    }

}
```

A referentially transparent function can be replaced, anywhere inside the code, with a constant that equals the functional expression's computed value:

```
4 === addTwo(2);
```

For example, this function is not referentially transparent:

```
function myJS()
{
    function addRandom(n1)
    {
        let number1 = Number(n1);
        return number1 + Math.random();
    }

}
```

Amongst the most notable JavaScript functions that are not referentially transparent and that generate side effects, we can mention these: `Date`, `Math.random`, `delete`, `Object.assign`, `Array.splice`, `Array.sort`, and `RegExp.exec`.

There are many advantages of keeping functions simple and pure. The most important ones are:

- Simpler critical paths, whereby the developer's cognitive burden is reduced when trying to maintain or update an application
- Easier testing of functions
- Free compiler optimizations, whereby a compiler might decide to replace a functional expression with its corresponding constant value at compile time, rather than computing the function each time
- Future performance boosts due to runtime optimizations
- Safe multithreading by avoiding race conditions due to application state mutability (JavaScript is single threaded for now, but who knows what the future holds)

Functions as first-class citizens

Functions as first-class citizens is a principle that states that functions should be considered to be just like any other datatype. When this is allowed within a language, functions can become higher-order functions whereby any function can be received as a parameter and returned as a computational value from any other function, just as any other datatype would.

When functions are pure and referentially transparent, they can more easily be used as first-class citizen functions. Thus, it becomes easier to combine functions together in order to dynamically produce other functions. This is what is known as function composition. Currying, by which a new function is dynamically generated to translate the evaluation of its single argument to another function with multiple arguments, and partial application, by which a new dynamically generated function with less arity will fix the number of arguments of another function, are the two main ways to combine functions together. As we will see later in this chapter, ES2020 is getting ready to introduce these concepts into the JavaScript programming language.

Dealing with side effects

What should we do with input and output, networking, user input and user interfaces if they are necessary to avoid all forms of side effects? According to FP principles, these interactions with the real world are to be encapsulated inside special data structures. Even though the contained value or values remains unknown until runtime, these special data structures make it possible to map a function to one or more wrapped values (functor), to map a wrapped function to one or more wrapped values (applicative) or to map a wrapped function that returns an instance of its own data structure type to one or more wrapped values (monad). This way, side effects remain segregated from pure functions.

Immutability

Another important principle of FP is immutability. Modifying state and data generates cyclomatic complexity and makes any computer program prone to bugs and to inefficiency in general. Indeed, all variables should, in fact, be immutable. A variable should never change its value, from the moment it is allocated to memory until the moment it is deallocated, in order to avoid changing the state of the application.

Since ES6, it is now possible to use the `const` keyword to define a constant or immutable variable. Here is an example of its usage:

```
function myJS()
{
    const number = 7;

    try {
        number = 9;
    } catch(err) {
```

```
        // TypeError: invalid assignment to const 'number'
        console.log(err);
    }
}
```

This added feature now makes it possible to prevent the modifications of variables through assignments. This way, it is possible to protect a JavaScript application's state from mutation during its entire runtime.

Whenever possible, the developer should always prefer using `const` over `let` or `var`. Trying to modify a variable that was declared using the `const` keyword will cause the following error (`chap8_js_const_1.html`):

Assigning to a constant variable causes a 'TypeError'

Functional programming techniques

Since ES6, JavaScript has made it easier to implement software solutions using FP. Many engine optimizations have been added that allow for better performance when programming JavaScript according to FP principles. Mapping, filtering, reducing and tail-call optimization are some of these techniques.

Map

Map is a higher-order function that allows us to map a callback to each element of a collection. It is particularly useful when translating all elements of an array from one set of values to another. Here is a simple code example:

```
function myJS()
{
    let array = [1, 2, 3];

    let arrayPlusTwo = array.map(current => current + 2);

    // arrayPlusTwo == [3, 4, 5]

}
```

This technique makes it possible to avoid using structural loops as much as possible when simply modifying the values of an array.

Filter

Filter is a higher-order function that allows us to distinguish and keep only certain elements of a collection based on a Boolean predicate. Of course, filtering is particularly useful when removing certain elements from a collection based on a certain condition. Take the following code as an example:

```
function myJS()
{
    let array = [1, 2, 3];

    let arrayEvenNumbers = array.filter(current => current % 2 == 0);

    // arrayEvenNumbers == [2]

}
```

Filtering is a great way to avoid loops and nested conditions in order to extract some desired dataset.

Reduce

Reduce is a higher-order function that allows us to combine elements of a collection into a single returned value based on a combining function. This technique is really useful when dealing with cumulative or concatenated values. In the following example, we are calculating the sum of the array's elements:

```
function myJS()
{
    let array = [1, 2, 3];

    let sum = array.reduce((cumul, current) => cumul + current, 0);

    // sum == 6;

}
```

Another FP technique that we will have a look at is tail-call optimization.

Tail-call optimization

In order to better understand what **tail-call optimization** (TCO) is, we will need to define what it is, understand how it works and learn how to determine if a function is tail-called or not.

What is TCO?

Tail-calling, or tail recursion, is a functional programming technique by which a function calls a subroutine function as its final procedure before returning control to its own caller. Direct recursion occurs when a function calls itself recursively. Recursion is mutual, or indirect, if a function calls another function which, in turn, calls the original function.

Thus, for example, when a function tail-calls itself, it stacks itself over and over again until a certain condition is met, at which point it will definitely return, thus effectively popping the entire call stack.

Optimizing tail-calls consists of popping the current function from the call stack before performing the tail-call and keeping the current function's caller address as the return address for the tail-call. Thus, the memory footprint of the stack remains small and stack overflow is in fact avoided altogether.

How TCO works

Let's compare two stack frames, one without TCO and the other with TCO. Let's have a look at the following code first:

```
function a(x)
{
    y = x + 2;
    return b(y);
}

function b(y)
{
    z = y + 3;
    return z;
}

console.log(a(1)); // 6
```

Once allocated to memory, without using TCO, the three stack frames from of the previous code would look like the following diagram:

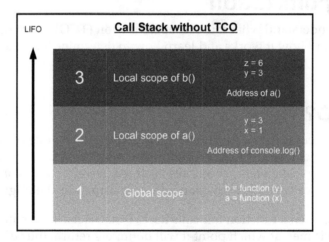

A typical last-in, first-out (LIFO) call stack

Once value 6 is assigned to variable z, the stack frame is ready to be popped. In this case, stack frame **2** is kept entirely in memory only to keep the address of `console.log()`. This is where TCO can make a difference. If, before calling `b()`, stack frame **2** were to be popped from the stack while keeping the original caller's return address intact, only one function would get stacked at any given moment at runtime and stack space would be reduced.

The entire stack would only count two stack frames no matter how many times functions would get tail-called. A tail-called optimized stack would therefore look like this:

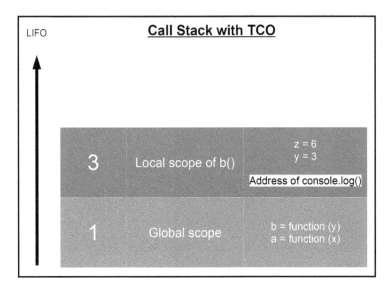

A tail-call optimized call stack

Some have stated that implementing TCO would be a bad idea in certain JavaScript implementations, as doing so would disrupt the actual execution flow of an application, make debugging harder and break telemetry software in general. This might be the case for certain JavaScript implementations, but it is certainly not true in the absolute sense. Technically speaking, implementing TCO might prove to be difficult due to technical debt in certain JavaScript implementations, but it is certainly not necessary to require a syntactic flag for something that should be implicit in any language, especially when using a strict mode flag.

This being said, not all browsers and JavaScript projects have implemented this ES6 feature yet, but it is a question of time before they will have to do it and developers should be ready for this major change. Indeed, this change from the structural to the functional paradigm will make it possible to make very efficient loops using functions rather than well-known loop structures. The main advantages of programming according to these new principles will be:

- Greater efficiency by consuming less memory and taking less time to complete large-sized loops
- Less cyclomatic complexity and simplified critical paths
- A reduced number of lines of code and less cognitive burden for the developer

- Encapsulated and well-organized code
- Better tested code in general

As of the time of writing, only Safari 11, iOS 11, Kinoma XS6 and Duktape 2.2 fully support tail-call optimization.

Let's take the two following code examples (`chap8_js_performance_1.html` and `chap8_js_performance_2.html`) in order to compare the performance of a traditional `for` loop with a tail-call optimized function. Here is the first example:

```
function myJS()
{
    "use strict";

    function incrementArrayBy2(myArray, len = 1, index = 0)
    {
        myArray[index] = index;
        myArray[index] += 2;
        return (index === len - 1) ? myArray : incrementArrayBy2(myArray,
len, index +
                                                                    1); //
tail call
    }

    let myArray = [];

    for(let i = 0; i < 100000000; i++) {
        myArray[i] = i;
        myArray[i] += 2;
    }

    console.log(myArray);
}
```

Here is the second:

```
function myJS()
{
    "use strict";

    function incrementArrayBy2(myArray, len = 1, index = 0)
    {
        myArray[index] = index;
        myArray[index] += 2;
        return (index === len - 1) ? myArray :
        incrementArrayBy2(myArray, len, index +
                                                1); //
```

```
tail call
    }

    let myArray = [];

    myArray = incrementArrayBy2(myArray, 100000000);

    console.log(myArray);
}
```

If we benchmark these two scripts, we will notice that there is not that much of a difference between the two, except that the one that uses tail-calls can be more easily unit tested, has a very simple critical path and could easily be memoized as it is still referentially transparent even if not pure for obvious reasons.

Here are the results for the first script:

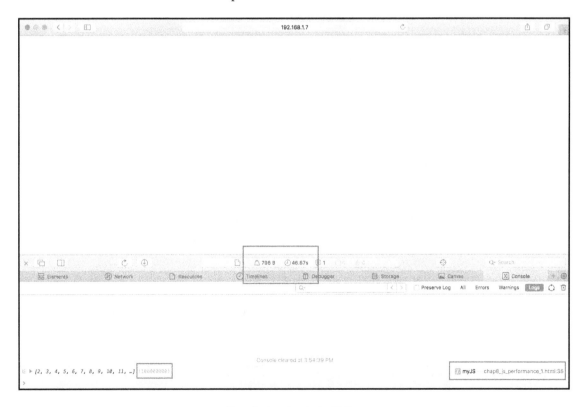

The results when using a structural 'for' loop

And, the results of the second script are:

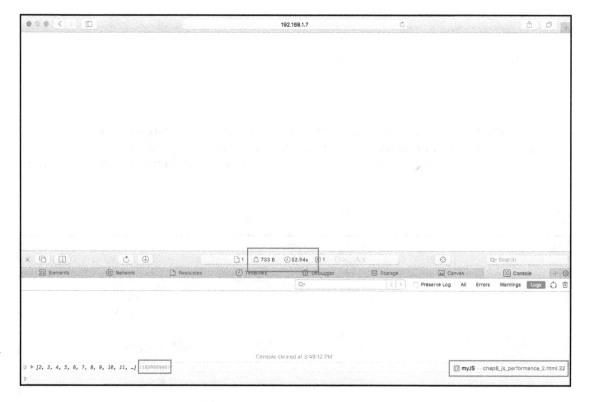

The results when using stacked functions that are tail-call optimized

Now, let's try to have a better grasp of this ES6 feature through a few code examples that will allow us to better recognize the different ways in which tail-calls can be used.

Recognizing tail-calls

As mentioned previously, tail-calls occur when a subroutine callee is called as the last procedure of the current function. There are many ways in which this can happen.

If you are using a ternary operator in the following manner, both the one() and two() functions are tail-calls:

```
function myFunction()
{
    // Both one() and two() are in tail positions
    return (x === 1) ? one() : two();
}
```

The following code example is not a tail-call, because the callee is called from within the body of the function and could be used to do further computation instead of simply being returned to the caller:

```
function myFunction()
{
    // Not in a tail position
    one();
}
```

Here is another example where one callee is not in a tail-call position:

```
function myFunction()
{
    // Only two() is in a tail position
    const a = () => (one() , two());
}
```

The reason is that the one() function can be combined with other computations in this context, whereas the two() function cannot and its returned value will simply be assigned to the a constant. The same would apply if we were to use logical operators instead of a comma as seen in this example.

Let's continue with other upcoming JavaScript features.

More upcoming JavaScript features

Many other features will soon be added to JavaScript that will push the language further down the road of functional and asynchronous programming. Let's have a look at a few of them.

Async functions

Because of asynchronous programming, the need for FP will be felt even more when generators will be used to do so and when avoiding race conditions will become even more important than it is now.

Indeed, ES2017 introduced `async` / `await` functions. These functions will allow us to easily create an `event` loop and make asynchronous I/O calls from within the loop in order to obtain non-blocking code. There will be many practical applications of this, including the possibility of speeding up web page loading times by asynchronously downloading complimentary JavaScript files after rendering is completed. Here is a code example using these types of functions:

```
async function createEntity(req, res) {
    try {
        const urlResponse = await fetch(req.body.url)
        const html = await urlResponse.text()
        const entity = await Entity.post({ // POST request })
        // More stuff here
    } catch (error) {
        req.flash('error', `An error occurred : ${error.message}`)
        res.redirect('/entity/new')
    }
}
```

Async generators and for-await-of loops

ES2018 defines the specifications for async generators and `for-await-of` loops. These features are already available in most browsers and will be of great help when programming asynchronously in JavaScript. They will mostly simplify the creation of queues and loops when iterating over async requests. Moreover, using async iterators, iterables and generators with async calls will be made very easy with the use of promises. Here is a simple code example using these new features:

```
async function* readLines(path) {
    let file = await fileOpen(path);

    try {
        while (!file.EOF) {
            yield await file.readLine();
        }
```

```
    } finally {
        await file.close();
    }
}
```

Pipeline operator

An ES2020 proposal is in the works to include more FP concepts such as easy function chaining using a pipeline operator. Thus, chaining functions will be made much simpler. Instead of doing something similar to this:

```
const text = capitalize(myClean(myTrim(' hAhaHAhA ')));
```

We would only need to do this:

```
const text = ' hAhaHAhA '
|> myTrim
|> myClean
|> capitalize
```

Partial application

A very important FP technique is also amongst the ES2020 proposals: partial application. As mentioned earlier, this FP technique makes it possible to fix a number of arguments to a function by producing a new dynamically generated function with less arity. Here is a simple code example:

```
function add(num1, num2) {
    return num1 + num2;
}

function add1(num2) {
    return add(1, num2);
}
```

The ES2020 proposal suggests that partial application could be performed as follows:

```
const add = (x, y) => x + y
const add1 = add(?, 1)
```

Of course, we could mention many other FP techniques that could find their way into the ES2020 specifications, such as function binding, currying and pattern matching, but what one must know is that JavaScript is increasingly becoming a functional language and that many future engine optimizations will automatically enhance overall performance of any executed code if it is written with FP principles in mind.

For further information on functional programming and functional JavaScript, please get one of the many good books and videos on these subjects that have been published by Packt Publishing in recent years.

Summary

We now have a better understanding of why JavaScript is increasingly becoming a functional language and how this programming paradigm can be a vector for performance. We have learned how replacing overly complex code with simplified functional versions and how using immutability and tail-call optimization can help make JavaScript more efficient. We also got a quick glimpse of the upcoming features of the JavaScript language.

In the next chapter, we will have a look at a few projects that have went along with Google's Faster Web initiative over the years and we will see how it is possible to combine these technologies in order to boost overall web server performance.

Boosting a Web Server's Performance

9

Amongst the main points that Google had identified as being the first order of business of its Faster Web initiative was to update the aging web protocols. Many projects around the world were already underway as the new focus of web development was shifting from offering more and more features to users, even if these were slow, to offering features that were not incompatible with web performance. Google's initiative helped to change web development priorities and, thus, allowed existing projects to come to light and new projects to be created.

In this chapter, we will cover a few projects that went along with Google's new initiative for the web. Thus, we will cover the following points:

- MOD_SPDY and HTTP/2
- PHP-FPM and OPCache
- ESI and Varnish Cache
- Client-side caching
- Other Faster Web tools

MOD_SPDY and HTTP/2

In 2009, Google announced it would start to find ways to update the HTTP protocol by making use of a new session protocol named SPDY (SPeeDY). This new session protocol worked over an underlying TLS presentation layer and allowed for many HTTP speed optimizations at the application layer. Using SPDY was as easy as activating SSL, installing the mod_spdy module on your web server and activating it. No modifications to the websites were needed in order to benefit from its features.

Moreover, all major browsers were supporting it. SPDY rapidly became a core element of the Faster Web and became, in November 2012, the basis of the next major revision of the HTTP protocol. Then, in 2015, it was deprecated in favor of the new HTTP/2 protocol. The most important optimizations that were introduced by SPDY and that would find their way into the new HTTP protocol's specifications were multiplexed and prioritized streams, server pushing and header compression. Let's have a look at each one of these optimizations in more detail before we get into some of the specifics of the HTTP/2 protocol.

Multiplexed and prioritized streams

SPDY's multiplexed streams feature allowed for mapping multiple requests to multiple streams on a single connection. These streams were bidirectional and could be initiated by either the client or the server (the server push feature). Opening multiple streams over one single connection made it possible to avoid the overhead of establishing a new connection on each client/server exchange, especially when downloading multiple resources in parallel to complete the rendering of a single page. Thus, this first feature made it possible to get rid of the limited number of possible connections when using the HTTP/1 protocol:

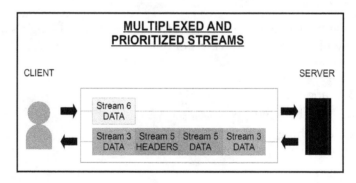

How multiplexed and prioritized streams work

Moreover, SPDY's streams were prioritized. This additional feature allowed the client to determine which resources should be sent over the wire first. Thus, SPDY avoided the **first-in, first-out** (**FIFO**) issue that arose when trying to do server pipelining (that is, the KeepAlive directive) within the HTTP/1 protocol.

Server pushing

As already mentioned, SPDY's new stream features made it possible for the server to push data to the client without responding to a client's request. This made communication bidirectional and allowed the web server to anticipate the needs of the client. Indeed, even before the client had done parsing the HTML and determined all the files that would be necessary in order to render the page, the web server could push the files down the stream to the client, thus reducing the number of requests sent by the client in order to fetch all the necessary resources:

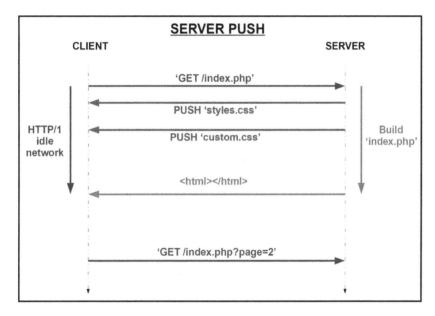

How the 'server push' feature works

By knowing that many studies show that, on average, most pages need from 70 to 100 requests against 20 to 30 domains in order to complete their rendering, we can easily see how this feature can make the web less verbose and reduce network latency in a significant way.

Header compression

SPDY's third important feature was header compression with `gzip`. By compressing the often high number of HTTP headers and reducing them by as much as 85% of their original sizes on average, SPDY could cut up to a full second off the load time of most HTTP transactions over the wire. Although the use of `gzip` to dynamically compress the headers was revealed to be unsafe, the idea of header compression remained and was re-implemented in the HTTP/2 protocol due to its great benefits to overall web performance.

HTTP/2

Published in May 2015 as RFC 7540 [1], HTTP/2 is the latest major revision of the HTTP protocol. It is mostly based on Google's SPDY protocol and offers a new binary framing layer that is not backward-compatible with HTTP/1. As mentioned previously, most of its features were developed through the SPDY project. The most notable difference between SPDY and HTTP/2 was the way that the new protocol compressed its headers. Whereas SPDY relied on dynamically compressing headers with `gzip`, the HTTP/2 protocol used a new method named `HPACK`, which made use of a fixed Huffman code-based algorithm. This new method was needed in order to avoid a problem that was found with SPDY, by which data compression led to the possible leakage of private data.

Even though the new protocol reduced the loading time of most web pages by as much as two times, many critics voiced their disappointment by pointing out that the unrealistic deadlines imposed by Google on the project of updating the HTTP protocol made it impossible to base the new version of the protocol on anything else but its SPDY project and, thus, causing many missed occasions for further improvement of the new HTTP protocol. *Poul-Henning Kamp*, developer of *Varnish Cache*, even went on to say that HTTP/2 was inconsistent and that it was overly and needlessly complex. Moreover, he stated that it had violated the principle of protocol layering by duplicating flow control that should normally take place at the transport layer [2]. Finally, many security flaws were found in this new protocol, the most notable ones being those unveiled by the cybersecurity firm Imperva at the Black Hat USA 2016 conference [3]. These were the slow read attack, the dependency cycle attack, the stream multiplexing abuse and the HPACK Bomb. Essentially, all these attack vectors could be used to bring a server offline by submitting it to a **Denial of Service (DoS)** attack or by saturating its memory.

Despite all of this and the many issues related to encryption, all major web servers and browsers have adopted it and now offer support for it. Most of the time, if your web server was configured and compiled with the HTTP/2 flag, you only need to activate the module in the server's `/etc/httpd/httpd.conf` file to start using it. In the case of the Apache Web server, you must also add the `Protocols` directive to the server's configuration files. Please be aware that activating the HTTP/2 protocol on your server will have a considerable impact on resource consumption. For example, enabling such a feature on the Apache web server will result in the creation of many threads, as the server will serve HTTP/2 requests by creating dedicated workers in order to process and stream the results back to the clients. Here is an example of how you can enable the HTTP/2 module in Apache's `httpd.conf` and `httpd-ssl.conf` configuration files (presuming that the `mod_ssl` module has been enabled also):

```
# File: /etc/httpd/httpd.conf
[...]
LoadModule ssl_module /usr/lib/httpd/modules/mod_ssl.so
LoadModule http2_module /usr/lib/httpd/modules/mod_http2.so
[...]


# File: /etc/httpd/extra/httpd-ssl.conf
[...]
<VirtualHost _default_:443>

Protocols h2 http/1.1

#   General setup for the virtual host
DocumentRoot "/srv/www"
[...]
```

For more information on the HTTP/2 protocol, please visit the following address:

- https://developers.google.com/web/fundamentals/performance/http2/

To learn more on Apache's implementation of the same protocol, please visit these links:

- https://httpd.apache.org/docs/2.4/howto/http2.html
- https://httpd.apache.org/docs/2.4/mod/mod_http2.html

And, finally, to know more about the implementation provided by NGINX, please consult their documentation:

- http://nginx.org/en/docs/http/ngx_http_v2_module.html

PHP-FPM and OPCache

When talking about the Faster Web, it is certainly important to consider how to make sure that the PHP binary itself is being run in an optimized way on web servers, considering that PHP is installed on seventy to eighty percent of servers around the world.

PHP-FPM

Since PHP 5.3, PHP now includes a FastCGI process manager that allows you to run much more secure, much faster and more reliable PHP code on web servers. Before PHP-FPM, the default way to run PHP code on a web server was usually through the `mod_php` module. What makes PHP-FPM so interesting is the possibility for it to adapt itself to the number of incoming requests and spawn new processes in a pool of workers in order to scale to the growing demand. Moreover, running PHP this way allows for better script termination, more graceful server restarts, more advanced error reporting and server logging, and fine-grained tuning of the PHP environment for each and every PHP pool of workers through the daemonization of the PHP binary.

It has been reported by many high-traffic websites that they have seen speed performance hikes of the order of 300% when changing from `mod_php` to `PHP-FPM` on their production servers. Of course, as Ilia Alshanetsky mentioned in one of his presentations[4], when serving static content, many other servers, like lighttpd, thttpd, Tux or Boa, can be as much as 400% faster than Apache. But, when it comes to dynamic content, no servers can be faster than Apache or NGINX, especially when they work in combination with PHP-FPM.

Enabling PHP-FPM on a server is as easy as configuring PHP with the `--enable-fpm` switch at compile time. From there, it is a question of determining how to run PHP-FPM, depending of performance and security issues. For example, if you are in a production environment, you might decide to run PHP-FPM with many pools of workers on many servers in order to distribute the workload. Moreover, you might prefer running PHP-FPM through a UNIX socket on the server rather than on the network loopback (`127.0.0.1`) for performance and security reasons. Indeed, a UNIX socket is always faster in any scenario and will offer better security against a local network attacker, that could always try to compromise the loopback with a socket listener using domain autorizations, by enforcing appropriate access controls to ensure connection confidentiality.

Zend OPcache

Since PHP 5.5, opcode caching is now available in PHP's core functionality when adding the `--enable-opcache` switch to the configure script at compile time.

Generally speaking, Zend OPcache will make any script from 8% to 80% faster. The more time a script's wall time is caused by the PHP binary, the more OPcache will make a difference. But, if the script's PHP code is very basic or if PHP is slowed down by latency due to I/O, such as a stream to a file or a connection to a database, OPcache will only slightly enhance script performance.

In all cases, Zend OPcache will optimize PHP script performance and should be enabled on all production servers by default.

Let's have a look at how we could configure the PHP-FPM server included with the Linux for the PHP container that is running PHP 7.1.16 (NTS) to use a UNIX socket, instead of the network loopback, to establish a connection between Apache and PHP. Moreover, let's configure PHP-FPM to use Zend OPcache.

Please make sure your container is still running and enter the following commands on its CLI:

```
# rm /srv/www
# ln -s /srv/fasterweb/chapter_9 /srv/www
# cd /srv/www
# cat >>/etc/php.ini << EOF
> [OpCache]
> zend_extension = $( php -i | grep extensions | awk '{print $3}'
)/opcache.so
> EOF
# sed -i 's/;opcache.enable=1/opcache.enable=1/' /etc/php.ini
# sed -i 's/Proxy "fcgi://127.0.0.1:9000"/Proxy "unix:/run/php-
fpm.sock|fcgi://localhost/"/' /etc/httpd/httpd.conf
# sed -i 's/# SetHandler "proxy:unix:/SetHandler "proxy:unix:/'
/etc/httpd/httpd.conf
# sed -i 's/SetHandler "proxy:fcgi:/# SetHandler "proxy:fcgi:/'
/etc/httpd/httpd.conf
# sed -i 's/listen = 127.0.0.1:9000/; listen = 127.0.0.1:9000nlisten =
/run/php-fpm.sock/' /etc/php-fpm.d/www.conf
# /etc/init.d/php-fpm restart
# chown apache:apache /run/php-fpm.sock
# /etc/init.d/httpd restart
```

You can now have a look at the modified `php.ini` file with the *vi* editor in order to make sure that the previous settings are no longer commented out and that the new `[OPcache]` section has been added to the file. Then, in your favorite browser, you should now see the following screen when visiting `http://localhost:8181/phpinfo.php`:

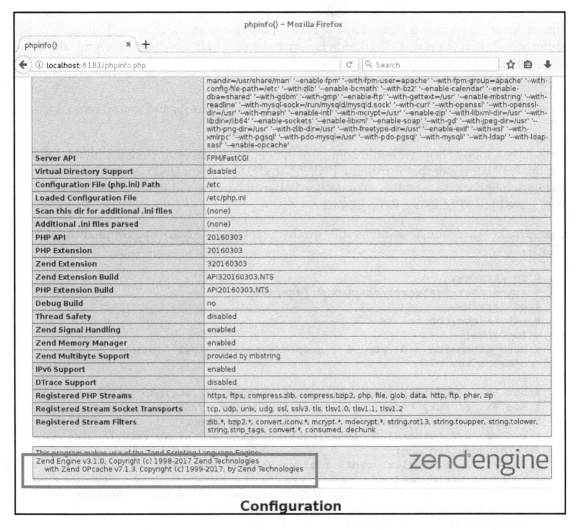

Confirmation that Zend Opcache is enabled and running

If you do see the previous screen, you have successfully connected the *Apache* server to PHP-FPM through a UNIX socket and enabled *Zend OPcache*.

If you wish to test compiling PHP from scratch with the FPM and *OPCache* configuration switches within a *Linux for PHP* base image (`asclinux/linuxforphp-8.1:src`), please enter the following command in a new Terminal window:

```
# docker run --rm -it -p 8383:80 asclinux/linuxforphp-8.1:src /bin/bash -c
"cd ; wget -O tmp http://bit.ly/2jheBrr ; /bin/bash ./tmp 7.2.5 nts ; echo
'<?php phpinfo();' > /srv/www/index.php ; /bin/bash"
```

If you wish to accomplish the same thing manually, please visit the *Linux for PHP* website for further instructions (`https://linuxforphp.net/cookbook/production`).

ESI and Varnish Cache

Another Faster Web technology is that of the **Edge Side Includes** (**ESI**) markup language and HTTP cache servers.

Edge Side Includes (ESI)

Originally formalized as a specification to be approved by the **World Wide Web Consortium** (**W3C**) back in 2001, ESI was thought to be a way of stepping up to the challenge of web infrastructure scaling by applying edge computing to it. Edge computing is a method of optimizing cloud computing by doing data processing near the source of the data instead of centralizing all data processing in the datacenter. In the case of ESI, the idea was to decentralize web page content to the logical extremes of the network in order to avoid having all content requests being sent to the web server every time.

The specification called for new HTML tags that would allow HTTP cache servers to determine if certain parts of a page needed to be fetched from the original web server or if cached versions of those parts could be sent back to the client without having to query the server for it. It is possible to think of ESI as a sort of HTML include feature that is used to assemble a web page's dynamic content from different external sources.

Many HTTP cache servers started using the new markup tags. Some **Content Delivery Networks** (**CDN**), such as Akamai, and many HTTP Proxy Servers, such as Varnish, Squid and Mongrel ESI, started implementing the specification over the years, although most did not implement the entire specification. Also, some of these servers, such as Akamai, added additional features that were not in the original specification.

Moreover, important PHP frameworks, such as *Symfony*, started adding ESI functionality within their core configurations, thus allowing the PHP developer to immediately start thinking of ESI when developing an application.

Also, browsers started encouraging ESI usage by keeping a local cache of all files that were fetched on the web and reusing them when a different website requested the same file, for example. Thus, using a CDN-hosted JavaScript file on your website brought the advantage of reducing the number of client requests to one's web server just to get that same file over and over again.

It is very easy to start using `esi:include` tags within your HTML in order to cache parts of your web pages. For example, you could use it in this way:

```html
<!DOCTYPE html>
<html>
    <body>
        ... content ...

        <!-- Cache part of the page here -->
        <esi:include src="http://..." />

        ... content continued ...
    </body>
</html>
```

Another example would be to use PHP and the *Symfony* framework to automatically generate the ESI include tags. This is easily accomplished by having *Symfony* trust the *Varnish Cache* server, enabling ESI in your YAML configuration file, setting the shared maximum age limit of the web page within its controller's method and adding the needed rendering helper methods within the corresponding templates. Let's go through these steps one at a time.

Start by having *Symfony* trust the *Varnish Cache* server. In the most recent version of *Symfony*, you must add a call to the static `setTrustedProxies()` method of the `Request` class. In the `public/index.php` file of your *Symfony* installation, add the following lines:

```php
# public/index.php

[...]

$request = Request::createFromGlobals();

// Have Symfony trust your reverse proxy
Request::setTrustedProxies(
```

```
    // the IP address (or range) of your proxy
    ['192.0.0.1', '10.0.0.0/8'],

    // Trust the "Forwarded" header
    Request::HEADER_FORWARDED

    // or, trust *all* "X-Forwarded-*" headers
    // Request::HEADER_X_FORWARDED_ALL

    // or, trust headers when using AWS ELB
    // Request::HEADER_X_FORWARDED_AWS_ELB

); }

[...]
```

Depending on the version of *Symfony* and the version of *Varnish* that you are using, you might have different steps to follow in order to do so. Please consult the following page of the *Symfony* documentation in order to complete this first step: https://symfony.com/doc/current/http_cache/varnish.html.

Then, add the following lines to your *Symfony* configuration file:

```
# config/packages/framework.yaml

framework:
    # ...
    esi: { enabled: true }
    fragments: { path: /_fragment }
```

Once done, modify a couple of controllers like so:

```
# src/Controller/SomeController.php

namespace App\Controller;

...

class SomeController extends Controller
{
    public function indexAction()
    {
        $response = $this->render('static/index.html.twig');

        $response->setSharedMaxAge(600);

        return $response;
```

```
        }
    }
```

And, the second one should be modified as follows:

```
# src/Controller/OtherController.php

namespace App\Controller;

...

class OtherController extends Controller
{
    public function recentAction($maxPerPage)
    {
        ...

        $response->setSharedMaxAge(30);

        return $response;
    }
}
```

Finally, perform the following modifications within your Twig template:

```
{# templates/static/index.html.twig #}

{{ render_esi(controller('App\Controller\OtherController::recent', {
'maxPerPage': 5 })) }}
```

You should now be able to see the effects of ESI when loading the pages of your *Symfony* application.

In order to get a better grasp of the inner workings of ESI, let's try installing and running an HTTP reverse proxy server that partially implements the ESI specification.

Varnish Cache

One of the HTTP Reverse Proxy Servers that partially implements ESI is *Varnish Cache*. This HTTP Cache Server was originally thought out by its creators, *Poul-Henning Kamp, Anders Berg* and *Dag-Erling Smørgrav*, as being a highly needed [5] replacement for *Squid*, a well-known HTTP forward proxy server (client proxy). It was possible to make *Squid* work as a Reverse Proxy (server proxy), but it was very difficult to set it up to act in this way.

The original meeting that led to the creation of *Varnish Cache* took place in Oslo in February of 2006. The basic concept behind the project was to find a way to quickly manipulate bytes that would be taken from passing network traffic and a way to determine what, where and when to cache those bytes. Many years later, *Varnish Cache* has become one of the most important HTTP cache servers on the web with almost three million websites using it in production [6].

In order to better understand how *Varnish Cache* works, let's take the time to install it inside a Linux for the PHP base container.

In a new Terminal window, please enter this Docker command:

```
# docker run -it -p 6082:6082 -p 8484:80 asclinux/linuxforphp-8.1:src
/bin/bash
```

Then, enter these commands:

```
# pip install --upgrade pip
# pip install docutils sphinx
```

You should now see the following messages on the CLI:

Confirmation that the requested Python modules have been installed

Then, enter these commands:

```
# cd /tmp
# wget
https://github.com/varnishcache/varnish-cache/archive/varnish-6.0.0.tar.gz
```

Once done, you should see a screen similar to this one:

```
                              vagrant@zend: ~                                 ×

  File  Edit  View  Search  Terminal  Help
3-1.22
root@488eb73358e2 [ / ]# cd /tmp
root@488eb73358e2 [ /tmp ]# wget https://github.com/varnishcache/varnish-cache/a
rchive/varnish-6.0.0.tar.gz
--2018-05-28 16:31:14--  https://github.com/varnishcache/varnish-cache/archive/v
arnish-6.0.0.tar.gz
Resolving github.com... 192.30.253.113, 192.30.253.112
Connecting to github.com|192.30.253.113|:443... connected.
HTTP request sent, awaiting response... 302 Found
Location: https://codeload.github.com/varnishcache/varnish-cache/tar.gz/varnish-
6.0.0 [following]
--2018-05-28 16:31:14--  https://codeload.github.com/varnishcache/varnish-cache/
tar.gz/varnish-6.0.0
Resolving codeload.github.com... 192.30.253.120, 192.30.253.121
Connecting to codeload.github.com|192.30.253.120|:443... connected.
HTTP request sent, awaiting response... 200 OK
Length: unspecified [application/x-gzip]
Saving to: 'varnish-6.0.0.tar.gz'

varnish-6.0.0.tar.g   [        <=>              ]   1.29M  1.29MB/s    in 1.0s

2018-05-28 16:31:15 (1.29 MB/s) - 'varnish-6.0.0.tar.gz' saved [1351443]

root@488eb73358e2 [ /tmp ]# █
```

The download of the archive containing the source code of Varnish Cache is completed

Finally, please finish the installation by unpacking, configuring and installing *Varnish Cache* with the following commands:

```
# tar -xvf varnish-6.0.0.tar.gz
# cd varnish-cache-varnish-6.0.0/
# sh autogen.sh
# sh configure
# make
# make install
# varnishd -a 0.0.0.0:80 -T 0.0.0.0:6082 -b
[IP_ADDRESS_OR_DOMAIN_NAME_OF_WEB_SERVER]:80
```

Once completed, you should receive the following message:

```
vagrant@zend: /workspace/projects/fasterweb                          ×

File  Edit  View  Search  Terminal  Help
root@ba6a0c2ccbf1:/# varnishd -a 0.0.0.0:80 -T 0.0.0.0:6082 -b 172.17.0.2:80
Debug: Platform: Linux,3.16.0-4-amd64,x86_64,-jnone,-smalloc,-smalloc,-hcritbit
Debug: Child (20) Started
root@ba6a0c2ccbf1:/# 
```

The Varnish Cache daemon is now running and waiting for connections

As we mentioned in `Chapter 2`, *Continuous Profiling and Monitoring*, of this book when we were installing the *TICK* stack through *Docker* containers, you can get the IP addresses of the two containers (the one running the *Apache* server and this new one that is running the *Varnish* server), by issuing this command:

```
# docker network inspect bridge
```

Once you get the results, you can replace the [IP_ADDRESS_OR_DOMAIN_NAME_OF_WEB_SERVER] placeholder in the previous command with the IP address of the container running *Apache* (the *Linux for PHP* container). In my case, the IP address of the *Apache* Web server is `172.17.0.2` and the IP address of the *Varnish Cache* server is `172.17.0.3`. The command would therefore be:

```
# varnishd -a 0.0.0.0:80 -T 0.0.0.0:6082 -b 172.17.0.2:80
```

Once started, you can point a browser to the IP address of the *Varnish Cache* server and you should get the *Apache* Web server's content. In my case, when pointing my browser to 172.17.0.3, I obtain the expected result:

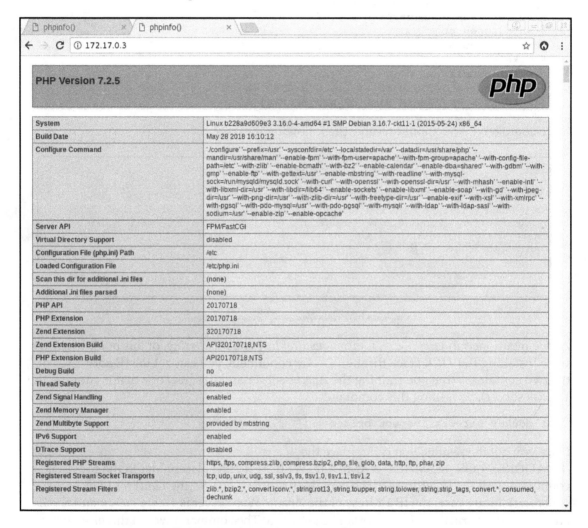

Varnish is caching and returning the response obtained from the Apache server

We can confirm that the *Varnish Cache* server is using our *Apache* Web server as its backend by issuing the following `curl` command in a new Terminal window and piping the results to `grep` in order to see the request and response headers:

```
# curl -v 172.17.0.3 | grep Forwarded
```

The result should be similar to the following screenshot:

The Varnish Cache headers are added to the Apache headers

As we can see, the headers show that the *Apache* server is responding via the *Varnish Cache* server.

Thus, with proper DNS configuration, it would become possible to redirect all the web traffic to the *Varnish Cache* server and use the web server as its backend only.

This example shows us how easy it is to configure a *Varnish Cache* server and how simple it is to start using it and benefiting from it right away in order to quickly boost web server performance.

Client-side caching

Let's continue with another Faster Web technology, which is client-side caching. This form of HTTP caching focuses on reducing the number of requests needed to render a page in order to avoid network latency as much as possible. Indeed, large responses often need many roundtrips over the network. HTTP client-side caching tries to minimize the number of these requests in order to complete the page's rendering. Nowadays, all major browsers offer support for these techniques and enabling these technologies on your website is as easy as sending a few additional headers or using library files that are already available on **Content Delivery Networks (CDNs)**. Let's have a look at these two techniques: browser caching headers and CDNs.

Browser caching

Browser caching is based on the idea that it is not necessary to fetch all the files included in a response if some of these are exactly the same over a certain period of time. The way it works is through headers that are sent by the server to the browser in order to instruct it to avoid getting certain pages or files within a certain timeframe. Thus, the browser will display content kept within its cache rather than fetching the resources over the network within the span of that certain period of time, or until the resource changes.

Thus, browser caching relies on cache-control evaluation (expiration model) and response validation (validation model). Cache-control evaluation is defined as a set of directives that inform the browser of who can cache the response, under what circumstances and for how long. Response validation relies on a hash token in order to determine if the content of a response has changed or not. It also makes it possible for the browser to avoid fetching the results again even if cache-control indicates that the cached content has expired. In fact, upon receiving the response from the server indicating that the content has not been modified, based on the fact that the sent token has not changed on the server, the browser simply renews the cache-control and resets the time delay before expiration.

This is accomplished through the use of certain response headers. These are **Cache-Control** and **ETag** headers. Here is an example of these received headers within a response:

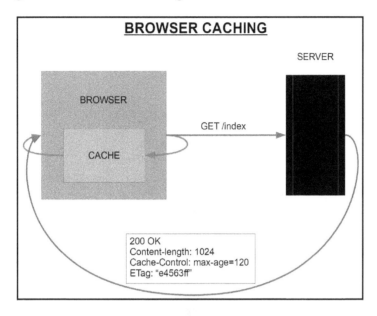

How browser caching works

In this example, Cache-Control indicates a **max-age** of **120** seconds and sets an **ETag** with value **"e4563ff"**. With these two headers, the browser will be able to manage its cache adequately. Thus, enabling browser caching is as easy as adding those response headers to the responses returned by the web server. In the case of *Apache*, it is a simple question of making sure that the FileETag directive was added to the server's configuration file.

It is also possible to set the Cache-Control and Expires headers directly using the *Symfony* framework in PHP. Specifically, *Symfony*'s response object allows you to set all Cache-Control headers using its `setCache()` method. Here is an example when using this method:

```
# src/Controller/SomeController.php

...

class SomeController extends Controller
{
    public function indexAction()
    {
        $response = $this->render('index.html.twig');
```

```
$response->setCache(array(
    'etag'          => $etag,
    'last_modified' => $date,
    'max_age'       => 10,
    's_maxage'      => 10,
    'public'        => true,
//  'private'       => true,
));

return $response;
    }
}
```

Having seen how easy and simple it is to start using browser HTTP caching, let's take the time to see how HTTP caching has other benefits to offer when combined with a technology such as HTTP Reverse Proxy server technology.

Content Delivery Networks (CDNs)

Content Delivery Networks are distributed networks of proxy servers that allow for high-availability and high-performance distribution of common or popular web resources. These resources can be web objects such as text, images and scripts, including CSS and JavaScript libraries, downloadable objects, such as files and software, and live-streaming or on-demand streaming media. CDNs can therefore be used as a sort of internet common cache. Indeed, by using a CDN to host all of your library files, you are combining browser HTTP caching with HTTP Reverse Proxy caching. This means that if another website or web application is using the same library files as you, your user's browser will either use its cached versions of the libraries or submit a request to refresh the files to a CDN and not your web server. This not only reduces network latency by reducing the number of requests needed globally to render the same content, but also takes away a part of the workload from your web server by delegating the responsibility of refreshing expired browser caches to the CDN's Reverse Proxy cache.

This Faster Web solution is very easy to implement. It is often as simple as redirecting web traffic to the CDN by modifying your DNS configuration. For example, *Cloudflare* (https://www.cloudflare.com/) does not require any changes to your web server configuration in order to start using its HTTP reverse proxy cache. Once you have registered the original domain name and IP address of your web server in the *Cloudflare* interface, you only have to modify your DNS settings by having the domain name point to the *Cloudflare* servers in order to start using it immediately. Let's use cURL to query the https://linuxforphp.net/ site, which uses *Cloudflare*:

```
# curl -v https://linuxforphp.net
```

Querying the website should yield the following result, which confirms that it is now only accessible through *Cloudflare*:

```
                              vagrant@zend: ~                              ✕

 File  Edit  View  Search  Terminal  Help
*          issuer: C=GB; ST=Greater Manchester; L=Salford; O=COMODO CA Limited; CN
=COMODO ECC Domain Validation Secure Server CA 2
*          SSL certificate verify ok.
> GET / HTTP/1.1
> User-Agent: curl/7.38.0
> Host: linuxforphp.net
> Accept: */*
>
< HTTP/1.1 200 OK
< Date: Sun, 18 Mar 2018 22:11:47 GMT
< Content-Type: text/html; charset=UTF-8
< Transfer-Encoding: chunked
< Connection: keep-alive
< Set-Cookie: __cfduid=d47a8f140e4522668511bb24655a0fd461521411106; expires=Mon,
 18-Mar-19 22:11:46 GMT; path=/; domain=.linuxforphp.net; HttpOnly; Secure
< Cache-Control: max-age=21600, s-maxage=21600
< Pragma: public
< Expires: Mon, 19 Mar 2018 01:41:43 GMT
< Expect-CT: max-age=604800, report-uri="https://report-uri.cloudflare.com/cdn-c
gi/beacon/expect-ct"
* Server cloudflare is not blacklisted
< Server: cloudflare
< CF-RAY: 3fdb09782b5a3fb9-YUL
<
```

Confirmation that the linuxforphp.net website is available through Cloudflare

As we can see, *Cloudflare* is indeed enabled and has added Cache-Control and Expires to the response headers.

Other Faster Web tools

Many other Faster Web tools exist that can help you optimize the performance of your web applications and websites. Amongst these many tools are those suggested by Google on their Faster Web site for developers (`https://developers.google.com/speed/`). One tool that will help you further analyze the performance issues of web applications is *PageSpeed Insights*.

This tool quickly identifies any possible performance optimizations for your web application, based on the URL you submit. To further analyze the effects of using *Cloudflare* for the *Linux for PHP* website, let's submit the URL to the *PageSpeed Insights* tool.

Here are the initial results before using *Cloudflare*:

Results of the performance analysis of the linuxforphp.net website when NOT using Cloudflare

And, here are the results after adding the *Cloudflare* reverse proxy server:

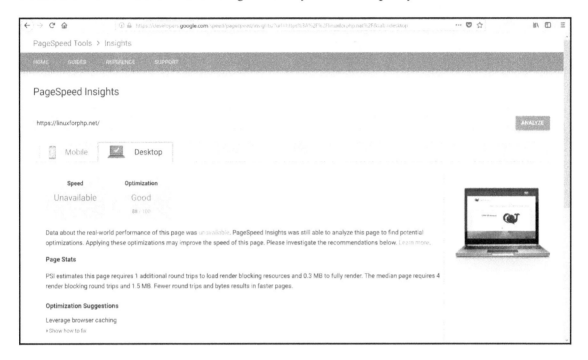

Results of the performance analysis of the linuxforphp.net website when using Cloudflare

Not only can we see that the general performance of the website is much better, but *PageSpeed Insights* also gives suggestions as to how we can further optimize the web application.

The initial recommendations of this tool, before the switch to *Cloudflare,* were as follows:

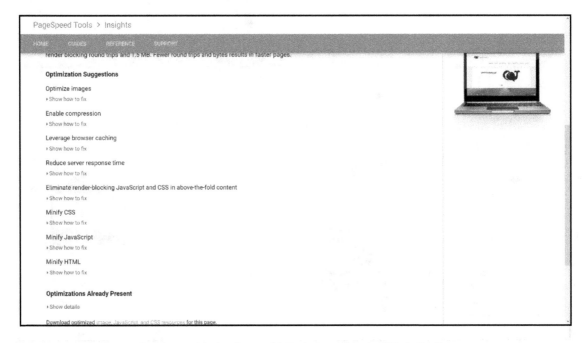

Suggestions to optimize the performance of the linuxforphp.net website when NOT using Cloudflare

And, then, after the switch to *Cloudflare*:

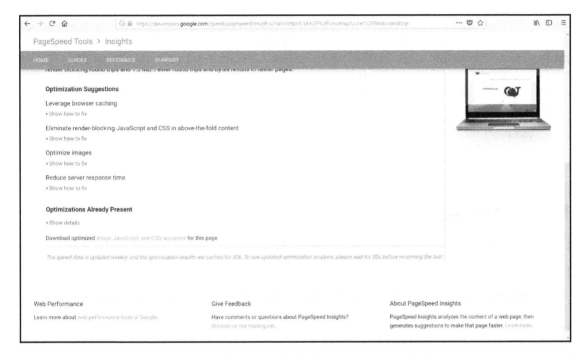

Suggestions to optimize the performance of the linuxforphp.net website when using Cloudflare

As we can see, the list of optimization suggestions is much shorter, but if we were to leverage browser caching for certain specific image files that can be found on the site, eliminate some render-blocking JavaScript and CSS, reduce image sizes and try to reduce server response time in general, we would most certainly get a perfect score!

Summary

In this chapter, we have covered a few projects that went along with *Google*'s new initiative of a Faster Web. We have seen what the HTTP/2 protocol is all about and how the SPDY project made it possible, how PHP-FPM and Zend OPCache can help you boost the performance of your PHP scripts, how to use ESI technology by setting up a Varnish Cache server, how to use client-side caching, and how other Faster Web tools can help you out when trying to optimize your web server's performance.

In the next chapter, we will see how, when everything seems to have been fully optimized, we can still go beyond performance.

References

[1] https://tools.ietf.org/html/rfc7540

[2] https://queue.acm.org/detail.cfm?id=2716278

[3] https://www.imperva.com/docs/Imperva_HII_HTTP2.pdf

[4] https://ilia.ws/files/zend_performance.pdf

[5] https://varnish-cache.org/docs/trunk/phk/firstdesign.html

[6] https://trends.builtwith.com/web-server, March 2018.

10
Going Beyond Performance

In `Chapter 1`, *Faster Web—Getting Started*, of this book, we mentioned that performance is also about perception. Indeed, as previously stated, time measurement depends on the moment of measurement and can vary depending on the complexity of the task to be performed, the psychological state of the user and the user's expectations as he might have defined them according to what he considers to be the software of reference when executing a certain task. Therefore, a good manner in which an application does what it has to do also means that the software would have to meet the user's expectations as to how this computer program ought to do things. Hence, quicker is not always better.

In this chapter, we will try to better understand the principles behind UI design when it comes to the perception of performance. We will see how these design principles can have a real effect on the user's subjective perception of time and improve perceived performance when there are no real optimizations left to do.

Thus, we will cover the following points:

- Clocked and perceived time
- Speed perception
- Reasonable delay and response times
- UI design principles and patterns
- Beyond performance tools

Clocked and perceived time

In the previous chapters, we have addressed the question of performance as it is measured by objective time. Objective time is measuring, by the means of a tool that divides, in equal units of measurement, a duration between an imminent future and an imminent past whose parts are in a continuous persistent flow of being.

This definition of objective time shows us that time is the effect of a movement of existence that takes us from an undetermined future to the state of a frozen past by the means of a constant present. It is objective inasmuch as a third-party being is used as a witness to this passing of being from one state to the other by dividing it into equal units of measurement. This is the reason why objective time is often named clocked time, as it refers to the concept of dividing time into equal units of measurement (for example, seconds, minutes, hours, and so on). Obviously, the field of science that studies objective time is Physics.

This being said, it is unquestionable that humans perceive the duration between two moments as being a variable thing. Indeed, we all know that time flies when we're having fun. In the field of psychology, subjective, or perceived, time is therefore defined as an impression left on the mind caused by the mind's level of awareness of the actual passing of time between two or more successive events. The more the mind is aware, the more time is perceived as having a long duration. The less it is aware, the faster time seems to pass:

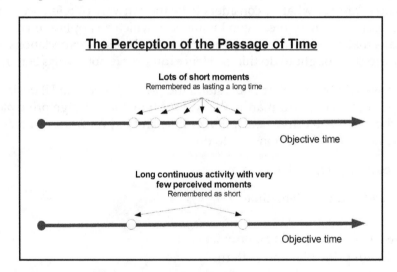

The passing of time as it is perceived by the mind

Many factors can influence how the mind perceives duration. Amongst the most notable ones are the emotional state of the person, the perception of the past and anticipated events, the general level of stress, body temperature, the presence of drugs and the general effects of age on the person's state of mind.

When applying these notions to computer science and more specifically to user interface design, the notions behind the study of perceived time become the principles that lead us to discovering how to influence a user's perception of duration and how this perception impacts the user's overall satisfaction.

Of course, many of these factors are beyond the control of the computer programmer, but there are elements to consider when designing user interfaces in order to positively impact user satisfaction.

Speed perception

Firstly, according to Paul Bakaus, a person's consciousness lags about 80 milliseconds behind what is currently happening. Indeed, the subjective present is always an objective past. Moreover, a person will need more time to understand and fully perceive current events if these are more intellectually complex in nature. These factors are true of any person. Thus, all users will unconsciously grant this free start up time for computer processing.

Secondly, the emotional state of the user has a strong effect on perceived time. In a fairly recent study by Awwwards and Google [1], it has been stated that anxious or rushed users will perceive more than 50% of websites as loading slowly compared to less than 25% for calm and relaxed users. This is equally true for users that are on the move compared to those that are comfortably sitting down:

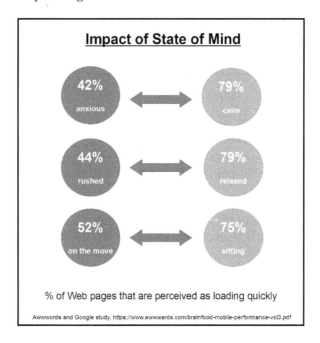

The influence of a person's emotional state or level of activity when it comes to speed perception

Thirdly, age is an important factor when considering perception of time. The younger a user is, the more he will be aware of duration. According to the same study by Awwwards, 18-24 year old users will only consider half of the visited websites as being fast, while 25 to 44-year old users will consider almost three quarters of the same websites to have loaded quickly:

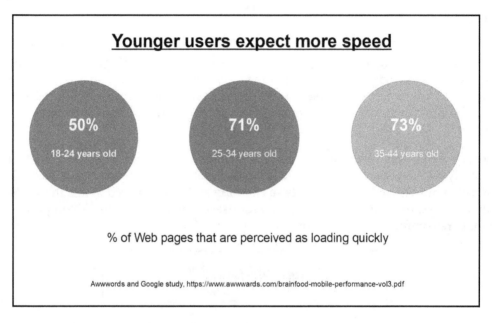

The influence of a person's age when it comes to speed perception

Lastly, all users will be less aware of duration when effective use of the application begins, even if it is not done loading. Slow retail sites often got high praise for perceived speed based entirely on the fact that users can start shopping for their desired items even though the browser has not completed the rendering of the entire page.

Thus, there are certain elements concerning speed perception that are common to all users and other elements that will depend on specific user profiles. It is up to the developer to discover these specific elements in order to have a better idea of how to make the best impact on overall user satisfaction.

Reasonable delay and response times

Another factor is what the user perceives as reasonable delay. As stated in Chapter 1, *Faster Web—Getting Started*, this is directly related to what the user considers to be the optimal performance of a certain type of application. This optimal performance is often determined according to what the user might consider to be an application of reference. In the case of web-based applications and websites, there are certain thresholds to be taken into account as they are shared amongst all web users on average.

Firstly, most users consider a response time of 300 milliseconds or less to be instantaneous. This is in great part explained by the previously mentioned "consciousness lag." As for response times between 300 milliseconds and 1 second, these are considered to be a reasonable delay and give the user the impression of a smooth transition. Many users will start losing attention and begin feeling impatient beyond a three second delay in response time unless there is some sort of user flow. Furthermore, a recent study by Google showed that more than 50% of users will leave a mobile website if its pages take more than three seconds to load. After eight seconds, user attention is considered to have been lost:

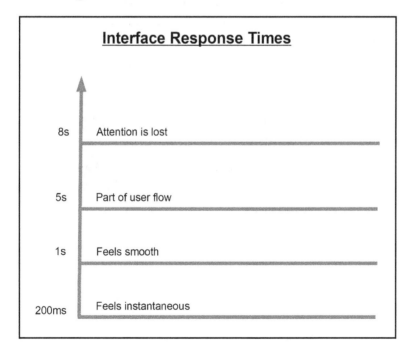

What most users consider to be a reasonable delay when using web applications or browsing websites

Secondly, all users that have accomplished a set goal or that have had a good perceived speed experience while visiting a website previously will be more forgiving and more likely to have a positive perception of duration when visiting the website in the future.

Finally, a positive speed experience will not only confirm user satisfaction concerning the website itself, but it will also influence the user's perception of the final outcome of the online visit and the overall appreciation of the business's brand.

UI design principles and patterns

Given all the previous factors and notions, certain UI design principles can now be abstracted and understood.

Firstly, speed is important to users. So, if no other optimization of your application can be done, make sure your users have the possibility to start using the application even before the initial page has finished rendering. This means getting to the **First Meaningful Paint (FMP)** of the page as quickly as possible in order to reduce the time it takes to get to the "time to interactive," which is the first moment when a user can start to interact with the application. One basic technique that can help you load the page's "above the fold" content before anything else is to place all blocking JavaScript at the end of the body of the page. Also, certain parts of the page can be cached for faster rendering or can be loaded in the browser through AJAX requests that are triggered with a periodical timer for example. Finally, HTTP/2's server push feature and HTTP Reverse Proxy servers could prove to be very useful when dealing with web pages that depend on many CSS and JavaScript libraries and frameworks in order to complete their rendering.

Secondly, even if a website is taking less than one second to load any of its pages, it is possible to speed things up a little more by removing the mobile browser's tap delay. This can be accomplished by adding an HTML meta tag in the head section of your pages:

```
<meta name="viewport" content="width=device-width">
```

Moreover, you could use the *Chrome* CSS rule in order to accomplish the same thing:

```
touch-action: manipulation
```

For older browsers, please have a look at *FastClick* by FT Labs (`https://github.com/ftlabs/fastclick`).

Optionally, since the pages are loading so quickly, it could be possible to add simple animations in order to make page transitions smoother. It would be best to ease in when prompting the user and to ease out when requiring an instant reaction through buttons and menus. These basic transition animations should last from 200 to 500 milliseconds, and when using bounce or elastic effects, one should think of transitions as lasting between 800 and 1,200 milliseconds. Even though these types of visual effects will give the user the impression that the application is a quality product, do not over-animate web page transitions and try to prevent content jumping when the page is loading unknown image sizes in order to keep the whole user experience as smooth and as streamlined as possible.

Thirdly, if your pages are taking from two to five seconds to load, it is recommended that you send some feedback to the users through the use of progress bars, throbbers or any other smart distractions. Also, make sure to explain what is going on by using simple expressions such as "% **of 32 MB uploaded**", "**Email is being sent**" or "**Estimated time left: 1 minute**".

Finally, if a page takes more than five seconds to load, you should get the users in active mode by getting them to play a simple game, for example. Of course, you can continue using throbbers, progress bars and display short messages to explain what is going on. But getting users into active mode will get them to be less aware of the passing of time. This is particularly useful for pages requiring very long loading times. Indeed, a very active user can completely lose track of time and become amused by a pleasant game at hand. This technique can also be used if you know that users will be anxious, rushed or on the move when viewing your application. Moreover, when pages require very long loading times, it should always be possible for the user to abort the operation and retry later.

This will also have a positive impact on the user's overall satisfaction, as it allows a user to be in full control of the lengthy operation:

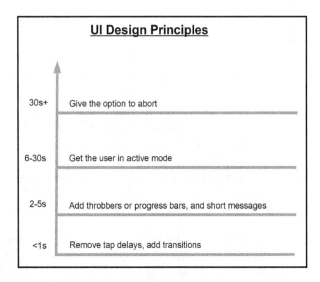

Applicable UI design principles depending on expected time delays

Now, let's have a look at how to implement a simple UI design using the previous principles and patterns.

"Beyond Performance" tools

In order to get a better idea of how to implement these types of solutions, we will create an animated transition that will wrap itself around a very slow PHP script. Thus, we will try to influence the perceived speed of the original script.

Our original PHP script will simulate slow execution by running a sleep command. Here is the content of the original script:

```php
<?php

// chap10_slow_before.php

sleep(5);

echo 'The original page loads very slowly...';
```

If we run this script immediately, we definitely perceive that the script is slow and that the elapsed time could make us believe that something is going wrong:

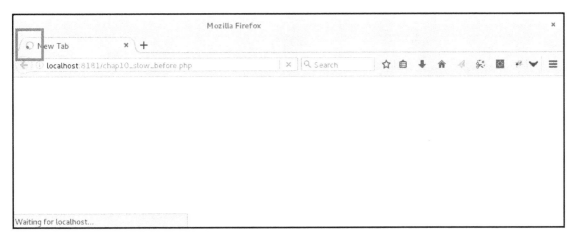

The script's slow execution might make us believe that something is going wrong

The script truly gives us the impression that it is momentarily hanging.

We will now create an HTML script that will query the original PHP script and obtain the script's output through an AJAX request. This new HTML script will also add some transition animations in order to influence the user's perception of the original script's speed.

In order to accomplish this, we will add a throbber that is entirely generated by CSS and we will use the jQuery and Modernizr libraries to do the AJAX call. These library files are hosted on CDNs in order to benefit from HTTP Reverse Proxy caching and browser caching. Here is the content of the second script (chap10_slow_after.html):

```
<!DOCTYPE html>

<html lang="en">
<head>
    <meta charset="UTF-8">
    <title>Slow page</title>

    <meta name="viewport" content="width=device-width, initial-scale=1">
    <style>
        /* Center the loader */
        #se-pre-con {
            position: absolute;
            left: 50%;
```

```
            top: 50%;
            z-index: 1;
            width: 150px;
            height: 150px;
            margin: -75px 0 0 -75px;
            border: 16px solid #f3f3f3;
            border-radius: 50%;
            border-top: 16px solid #3498db;
            width: 120px;
            height: 120px;
            -webkit-animation: spin 2s linear infinite;
            animation: spin 2s linear infinite;
        }

        @-webkit-keyframes spin {
            0% { -webkit-transform: rotate(0deg); }
            100% { -webkit-transform: rotate(360deg); }
        }

        @keyframes spin {
            0% { transform: rotate(0deg); }
            100% { transform: rotate(360deg); }
        }

        /* Add animation to "page content" */
        .animate-bottom {
            position: relative;
            -webkit-animation-name: animatebottom;
            -webkit-animation-duration: 1s;
            animation-name: animatebottom;
            animation-duration: 1s;
        }

        @-webkit-keyframes animatebottom {
            from { bottom:-100px; opacity:0 }
            to { bottom:0px; opacity:1 }
        }

        @keyframes animatebottom {
            from{ bottom:-100px; opacity:0 }
            to{ bottom:0; opacity:1 }
        }

        #contents {
            display: none;
            text-align: left;
        }
    </style>
```

```
</head>

<body onload="myAnimatedAjax()" style="margin:0;">

<div id="se-pre-con"></div>

<div id="contents"></div>

<script type="text/javascript"
src="http://ajax.googleapis.com/ajax/libs/jquery/1.5.2/jquery.min.js"></scr
ipt>
<script type="text/javascript"
src="http://cdnjs.cloudflare.com/ajax/libs/modernizr/2.8.2/modernizr.js"></
script>

<script type="text/javascript">

    jQuery.ajaxSetup({
        beforeSend: function() {
            $("#contents").html("Loading page... One moment
please...").toggle();
        },
        complete: function(){
            $("#se-pre-con").fadeOut("slow"); //toggle visibility: off
        },
        success: function(result) {
            $("#contents").html(result);
        }
    });

    function myAnimatedAjax() {
        var myVar = setTimeout(animatedAjax, 500);
    }

    function animatedAjax() {
        $.ajax({
            type: "GET",
            url: "/chap10_slow_before.php"
        });
    }

</script>

</body>

</html>
```

When running this new script, you should see a throbber appear:

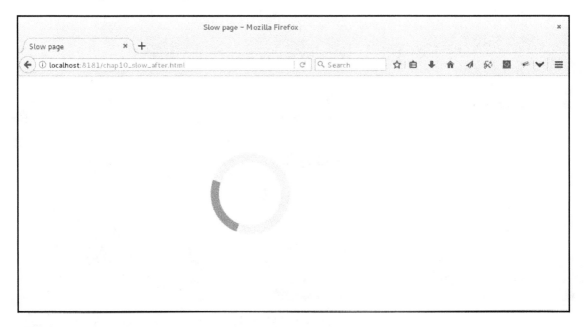

The throbber informs the user that something is happening.

And then, a few moments later, you will see a message stating that the desired page is being loaded:

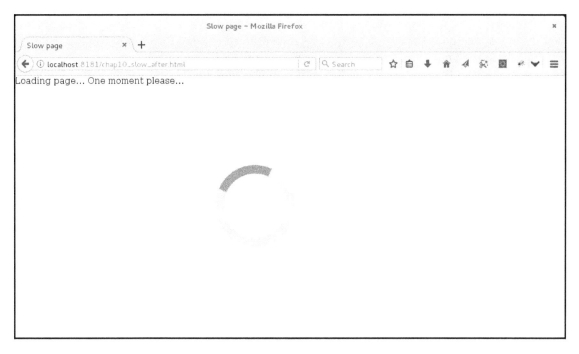

The new message distracts the user and partially resets the user's perception of the passing of time

This new message aims to distract the user and causes the user's perception of time to be partially reset. Finally, when the AJAX request is completed, the throbber and the message both disappear in order to display the other page's content:

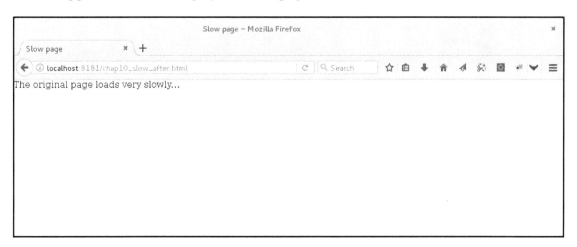

The throbber and the message both disappear and the original script's output is displayed

When letting the new script run, we definitely get the impression that the original script's wall time has decreased when, in fact, it has increased due to the 0.5 second timeout that was added to the JavaScript function that is making the AJAX request. If you run the JavaScript profiler that we mentioned in previous chapters on this new script, you will get to see what is happening behind the scenes:

Most of the execution time (six seconds) is passed waiting for the original script to complete its execution

The profiler confirms that most of this script's wall time is explained by the network I/O to the original script that takes as much time as before to load. But what we have achieved with the new wrapper script is giving the impression to the end user that we have succeeded in going "beyond performance."

Summary

In this chapter, we have better understood the principles behind UI design when it comes to the perception of performance. We have seen how these design principles can have a real effect on the user's subjective perception of time and how they can improve perceived performance when there are no real optimizations left to do.

We hope that you have found this book useful to better understand the notions of performance and efficiency, to discover most of the new underlying web technologies that make up what the Internet has become today and to help you on your way to mastering the Faster Web.

References

[1] https://www.awwwards.com/brainfood-mobile-performance-vol3.pdf

Other Books You May Enjoy

If you enjoyed this book, you may be interested in these other books by Packt:

Mastering PHP 7
Branko Ajzele

ISBN: 9781785882814

- Grasp the current state of PHP language and the PHP standards
- Effectively implement logging and error handling during development
- Build services through SOAP and REST and Apache Trift
- Get to know the benefits of serverless architecture
- Understand the basic principles of reactive programming to write asynchronous code
- Practically implement several important design patterns
- Write efficient code by executing dependency injection
- See the working of all magic methods
- Handle the command-line area tools and processes
- Control the development process with proper debugging and profiling

Building RESTful Web Services with PHP 7
Haafiz Waheed-ud-din Ahmad

ISBN: 9781787127746

- Understand the REST API architecture and its benefits
- Write RESTful API web services in PHP 7
- Address security-elated issues in a REST API
- Leverage the importance of automated testing and write tests for API endpoints
- Identify security flaws in our current API endpoints and tackle them effectively
- Observe the working of Lumen microframeworks and write RESTful web services in it

Leave a review - let other readers know what you think

Please share your thoughts on this book with others by leaving a review on the site that you bought it from. If you purchased the book from Amazon, please leave us an honest review on this book's Amazon page. This is vital so that other potential readers can see and use your unbiased opinion to make purchasing decisions, we can understand what our customers think about our products, and our authors can see your feedback on the title that they have worked with Packt to create. It will only take a few minutes of your time, but is valuable to other potential customers, our authors, and Packt. Thank you!

Index

www.ingramcontent.com/pod-product-compliance
Lightning Source LLC
Chambersburg PA
CBHW080632060326
40690CB00021B/4903